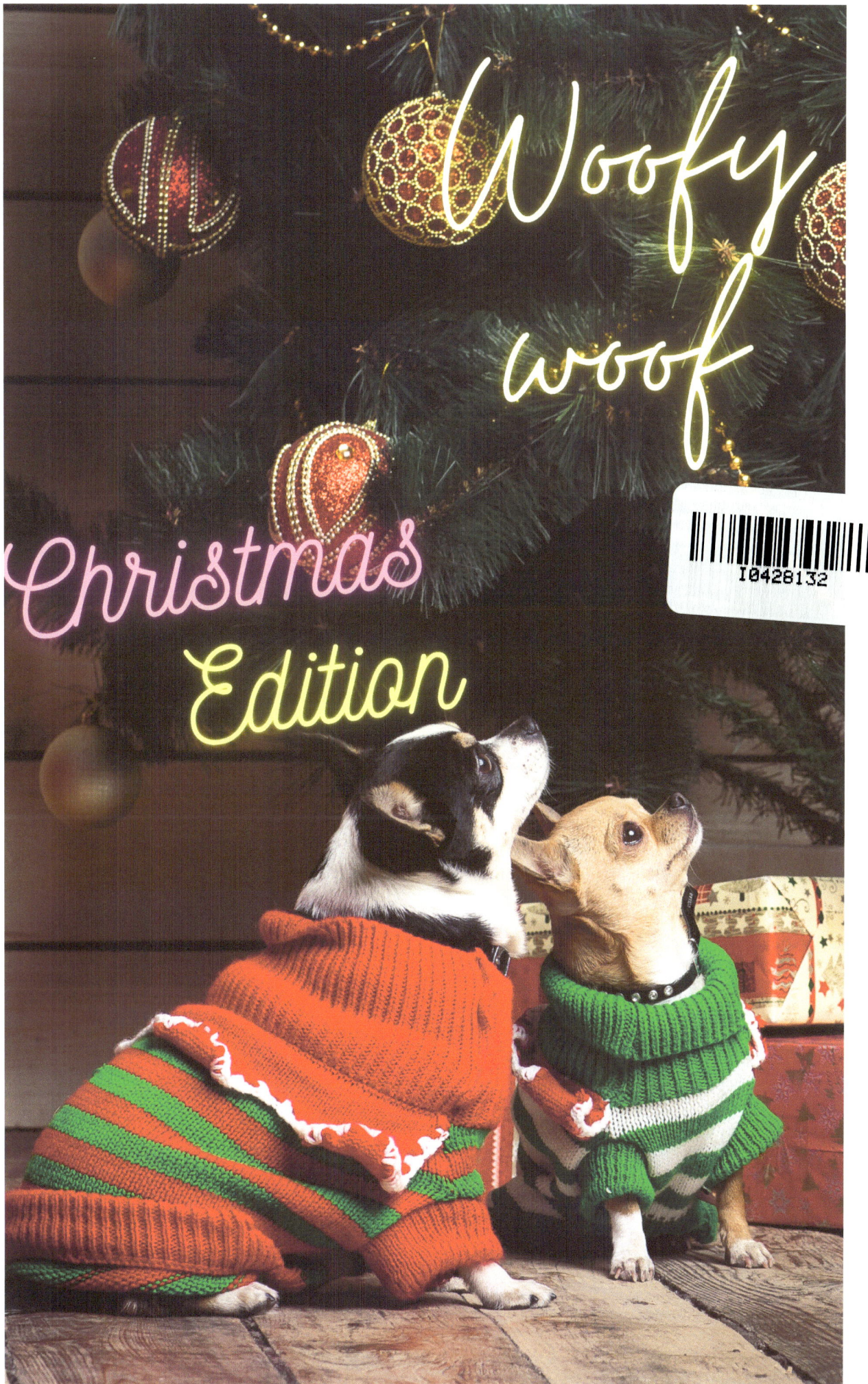

Woofy woof

Christmas Edition

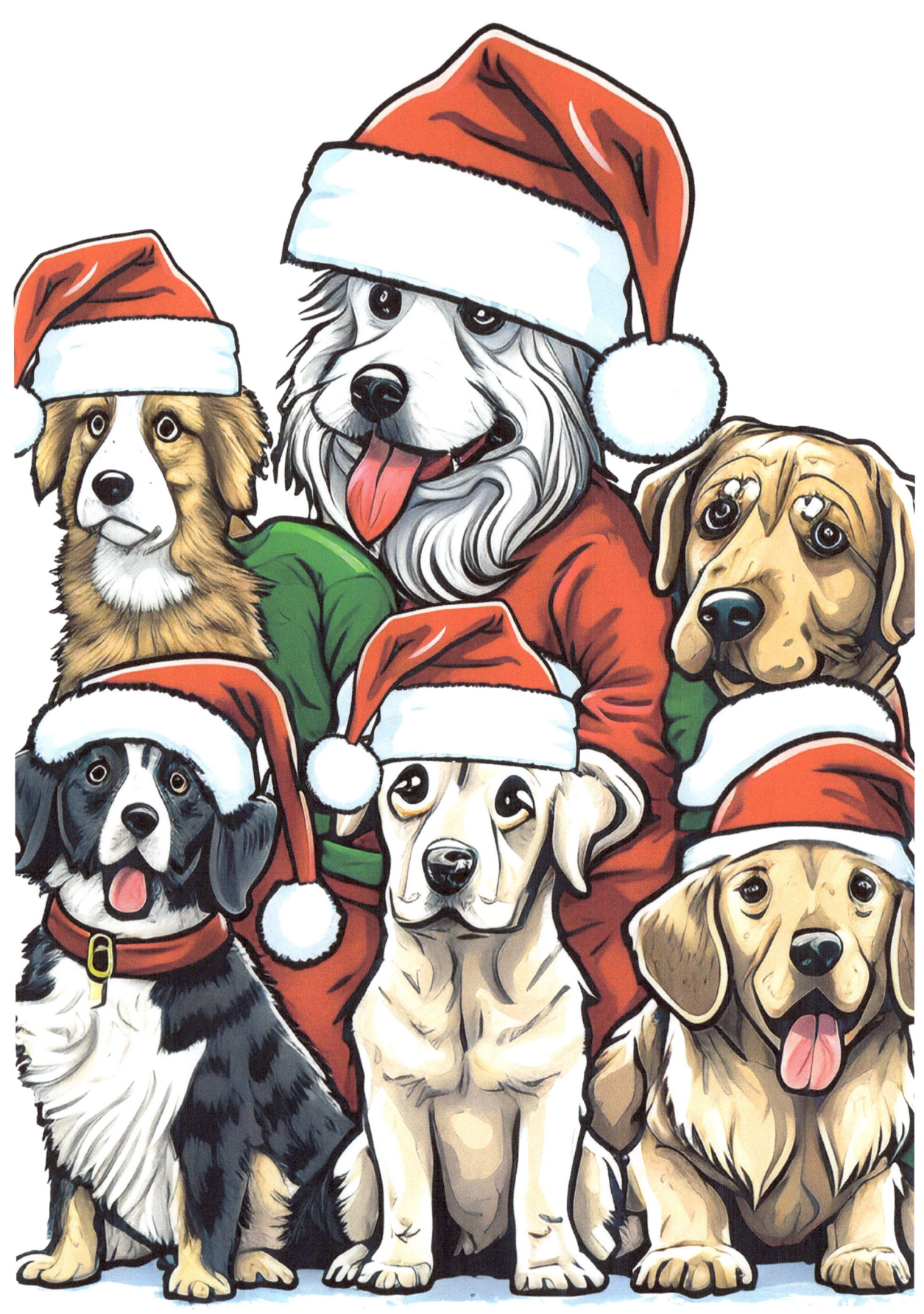

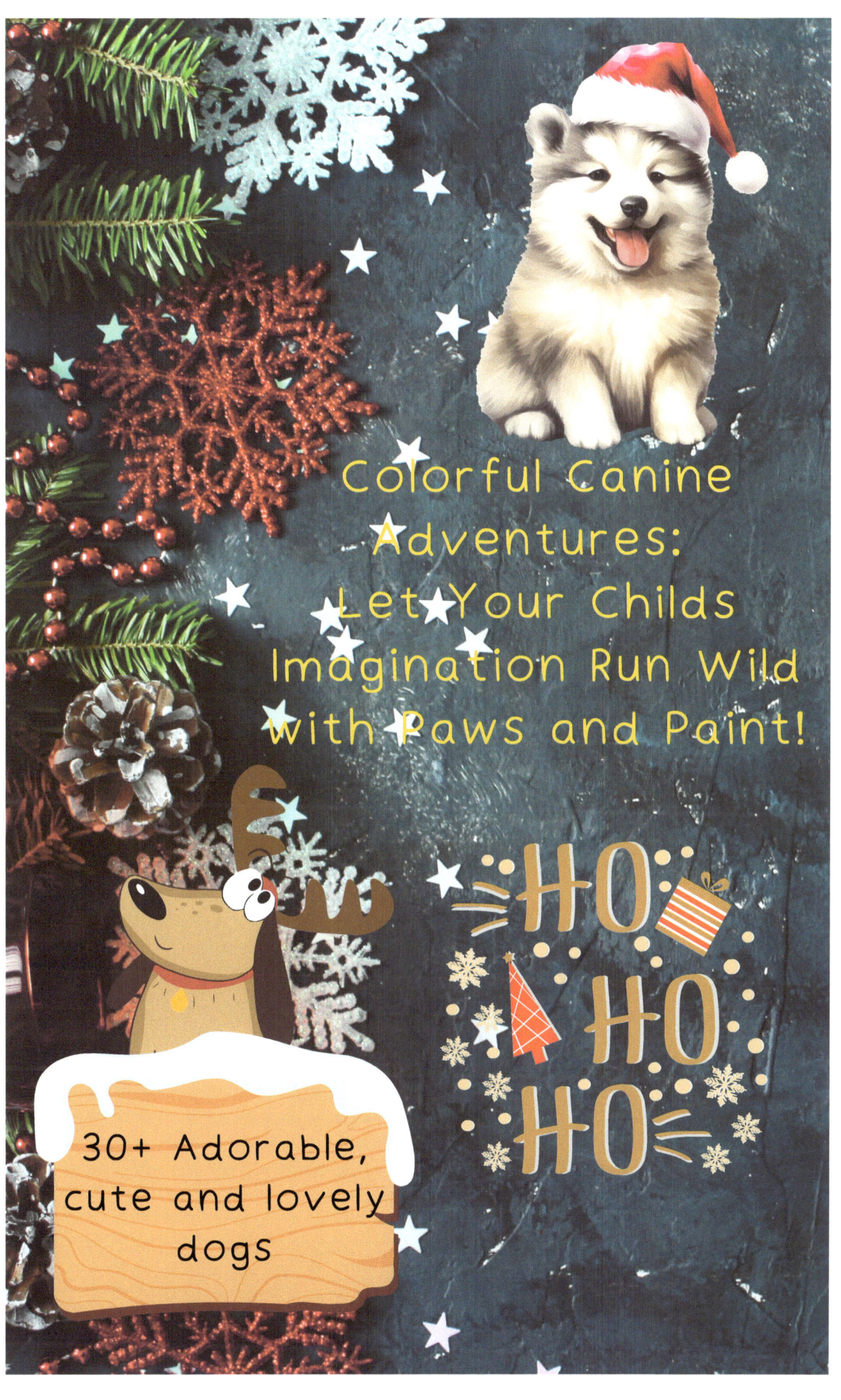

Colorful Canine Adventures: Let Your Childs Imagination Run Wild With Paws and Paint!

HO HO HO

30+ Adorable, cute and lovely dogs

❀ Bichon

With a fluffy white coat that's oh so fine,
The Bichon prances with a cheerful shine.
Their friendly nature and joyful zest,
Make them a delightful furry guest.

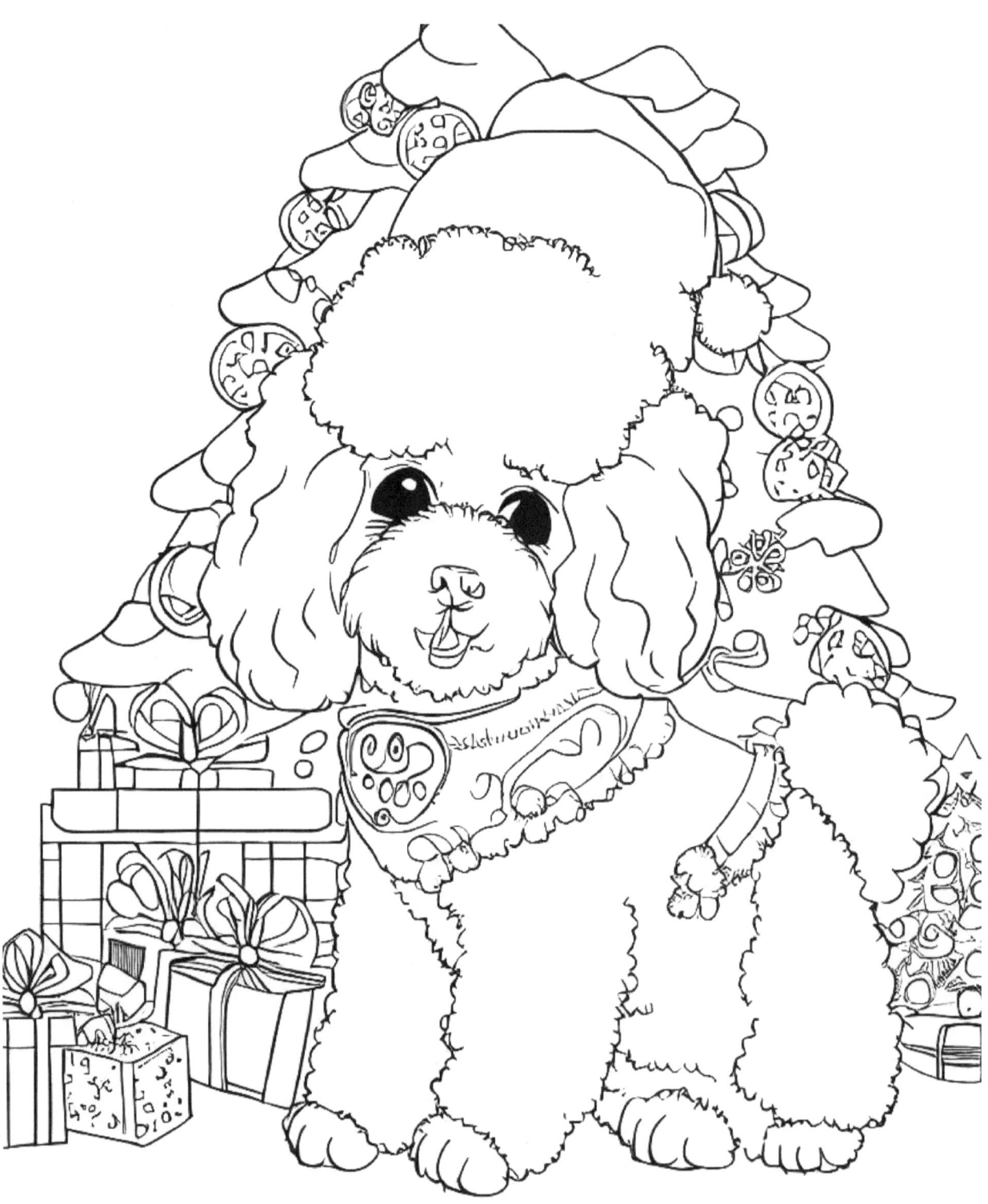

❤ Akita

In mountains of grace, the Akita roams,
A loyal companion, in regal tones.
Fur like soft silk, a guardian true,
A breed of honor, in eyes of amber hue..

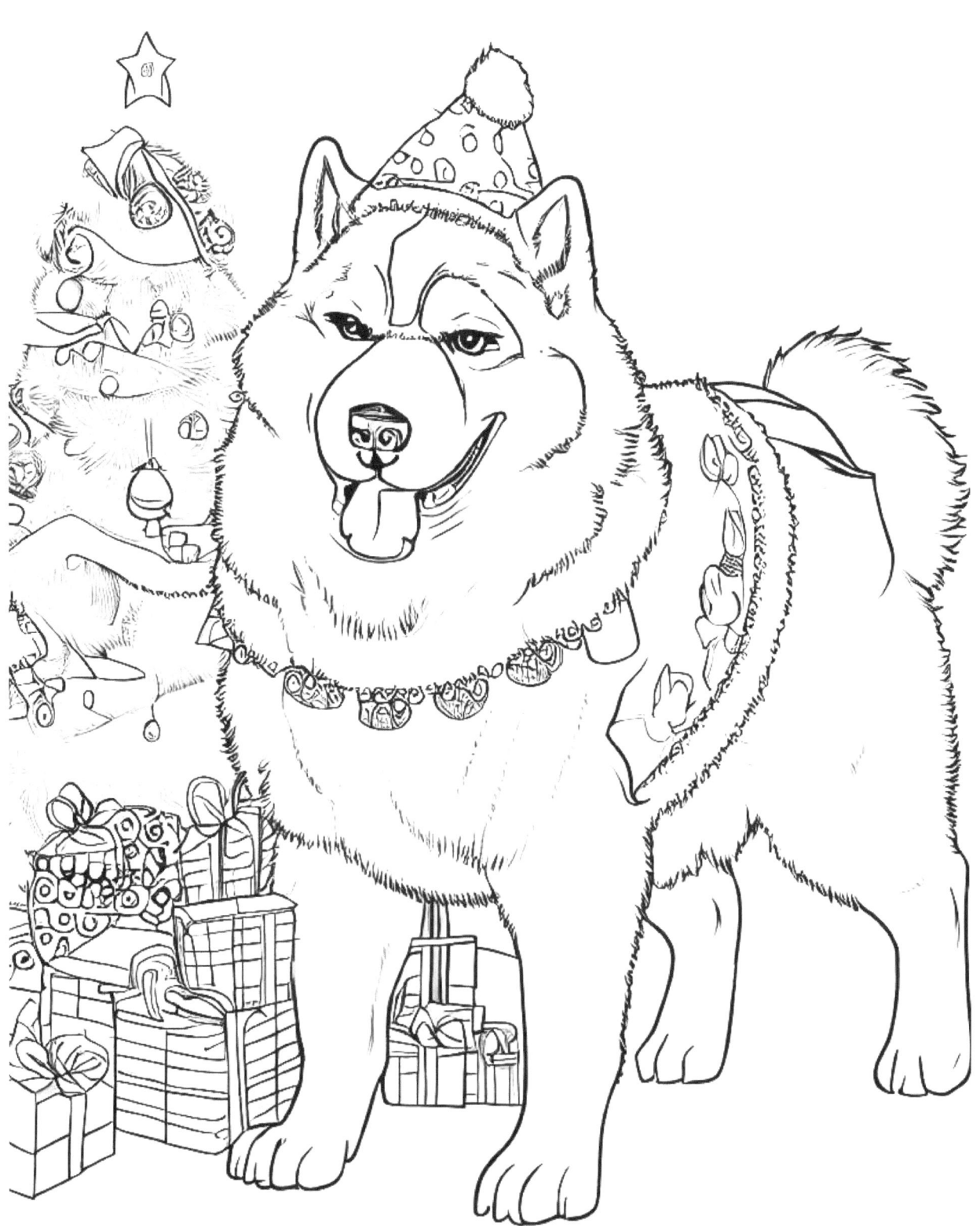

✿ Australian Shepherd

In the land down under, where kangaroos hop,
Lives the Australian Shepherd, a shepherd with a lot of pop.
With a coat so colorful and eyes so bright,
This herding dog shines with intelligence and might.

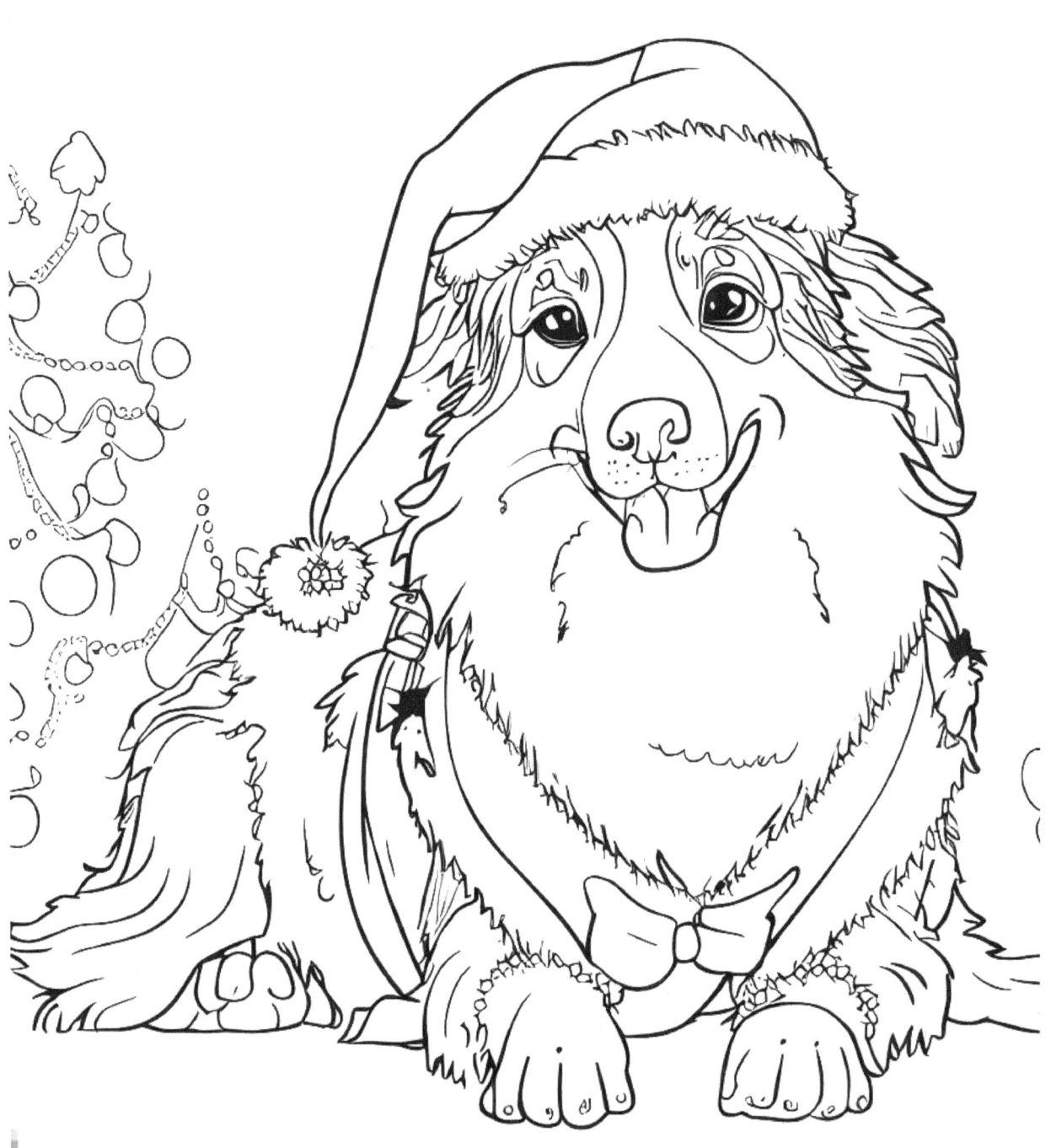

❀ Basset Hound

In a world of sniffs and long floppy ears,
The Basset Hound waddles without any fears.
With a soulful gaze and a nose that's keen,
This lovable breed is a sight to be seen.

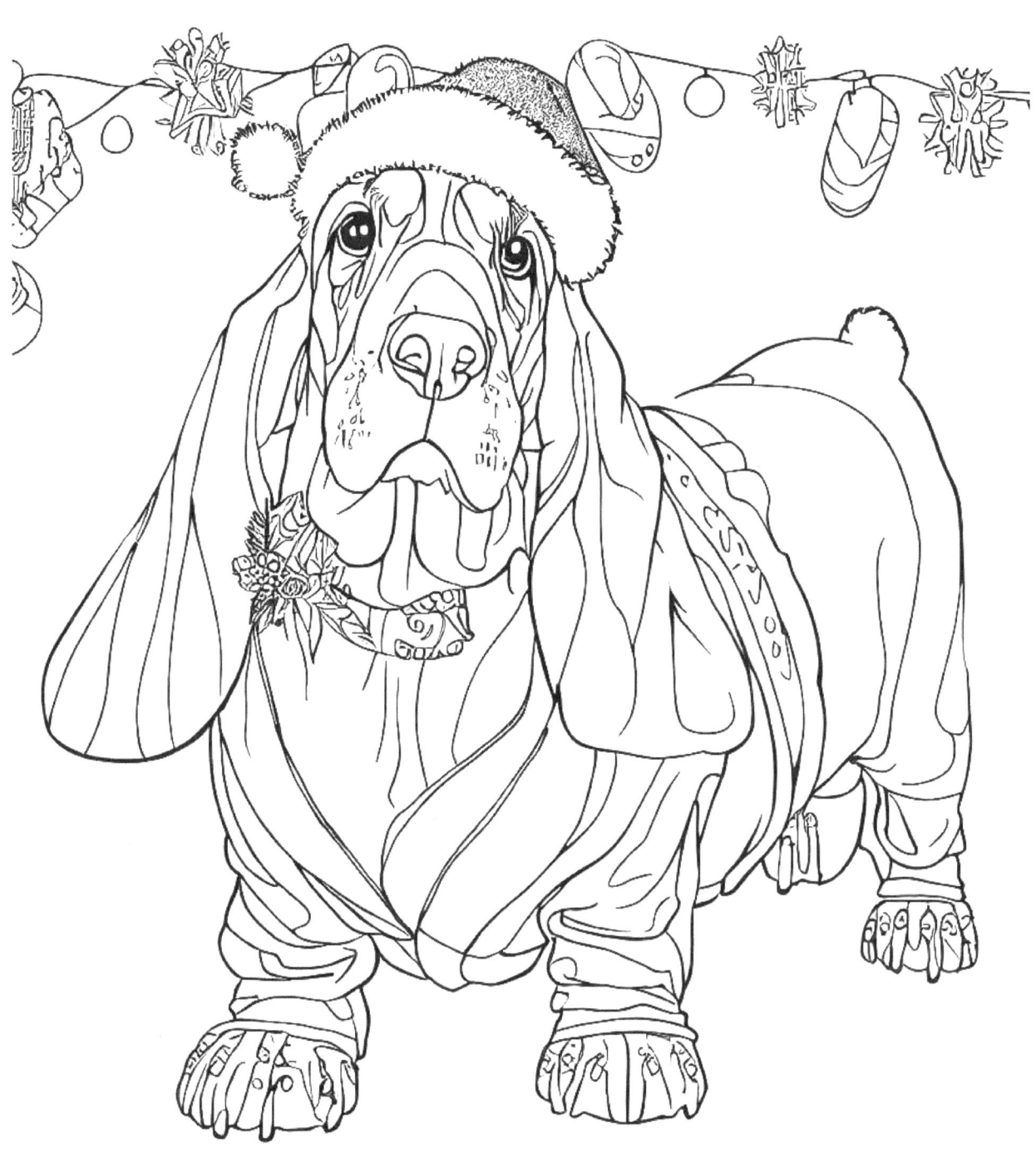

✿ Beagle

In the meadows and fields, where adventure abounds,
The Beagles are barking, following scent trails that astound.
With wagging tails and ears that flop,
These playful pups never want to stop.

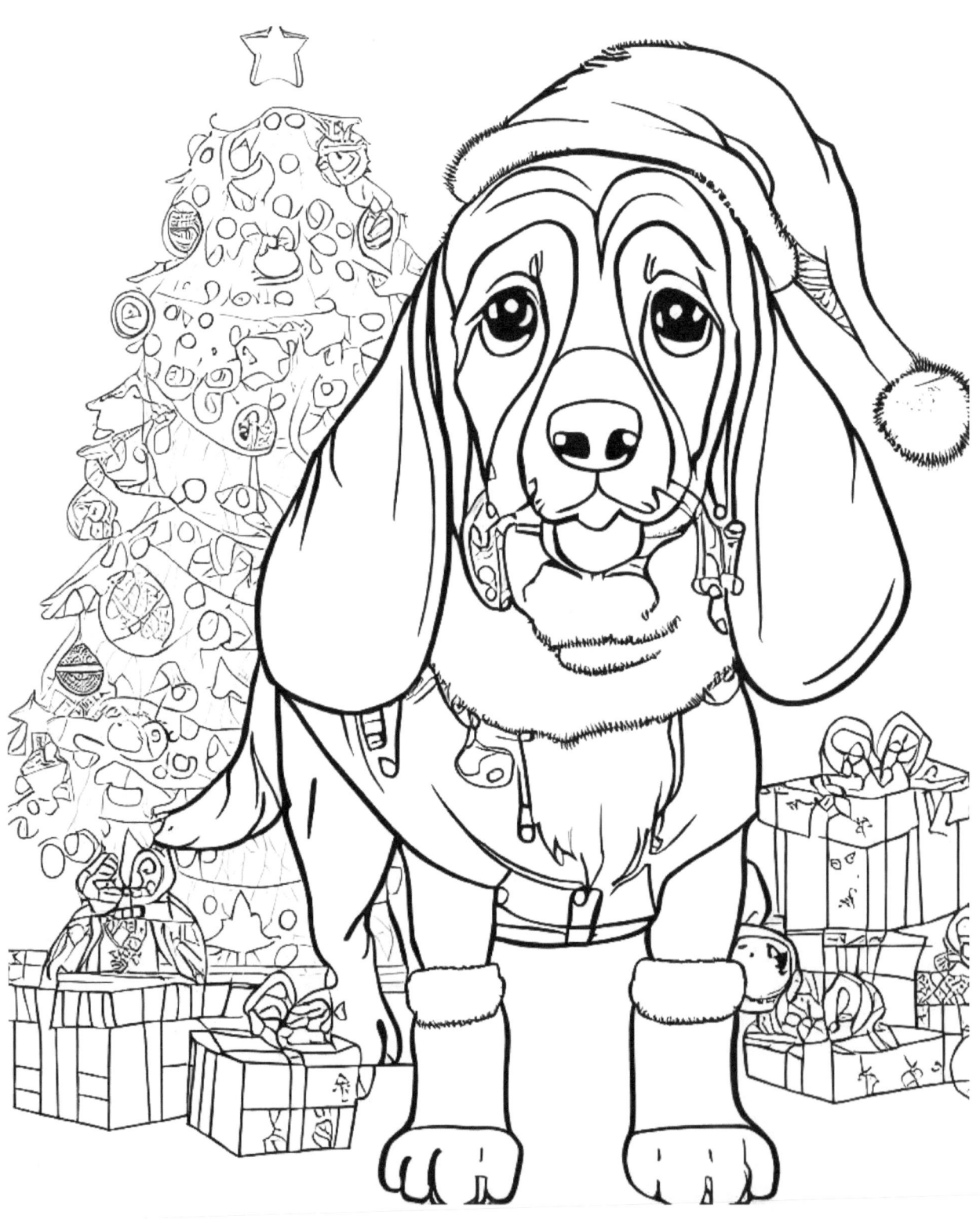

✿ Bernese

Gentle giant, strong and true,
With a heart as big as the sky so blue.
Among the mountains, they find their place,
A loyal companion to embrace.

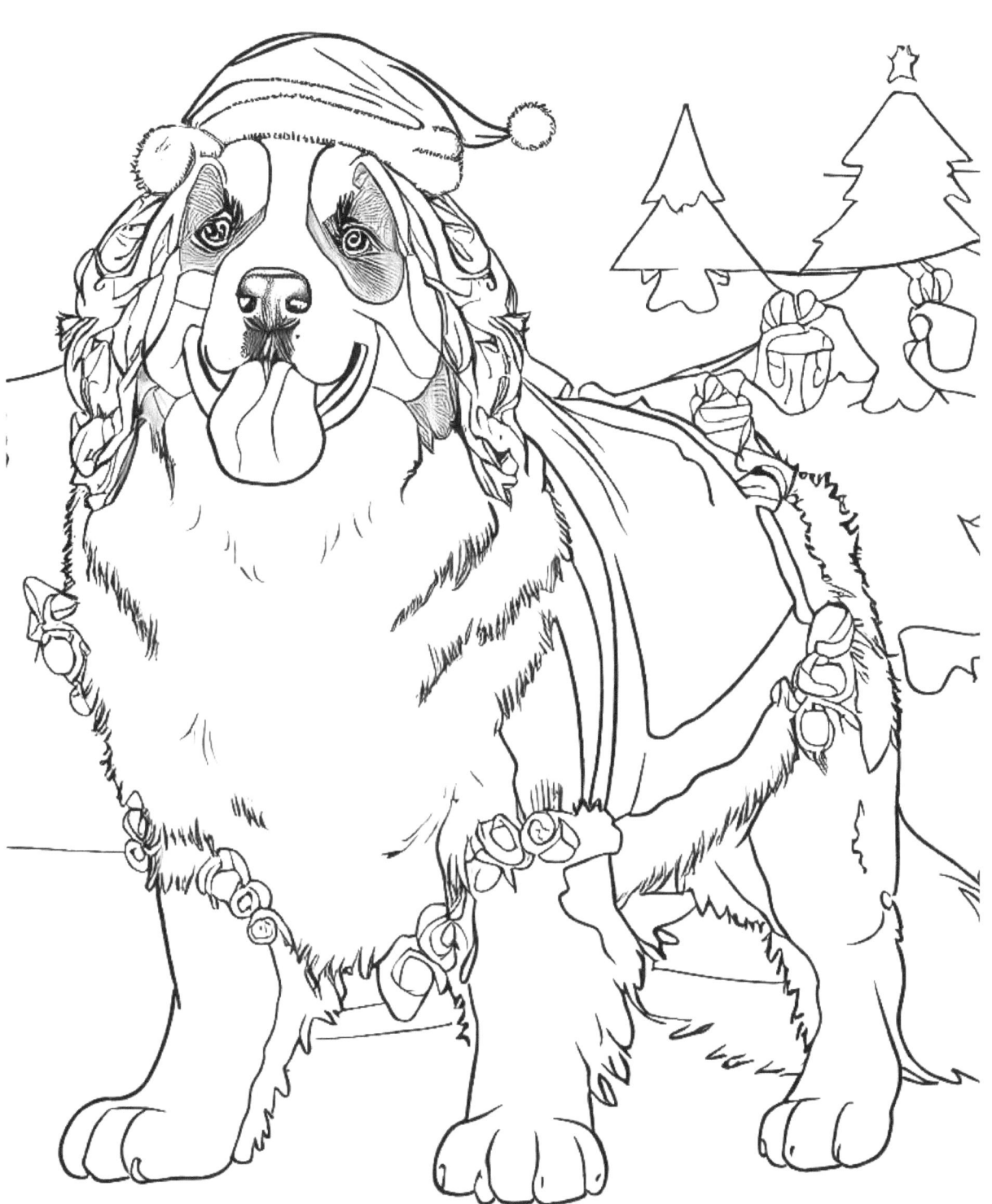

❀ Boston Terrier

Tuxedoed in black and white,
Boston Terrier's a playful sight.
With a snort and a joyful bark,
They'll light up your life, even in the dark.

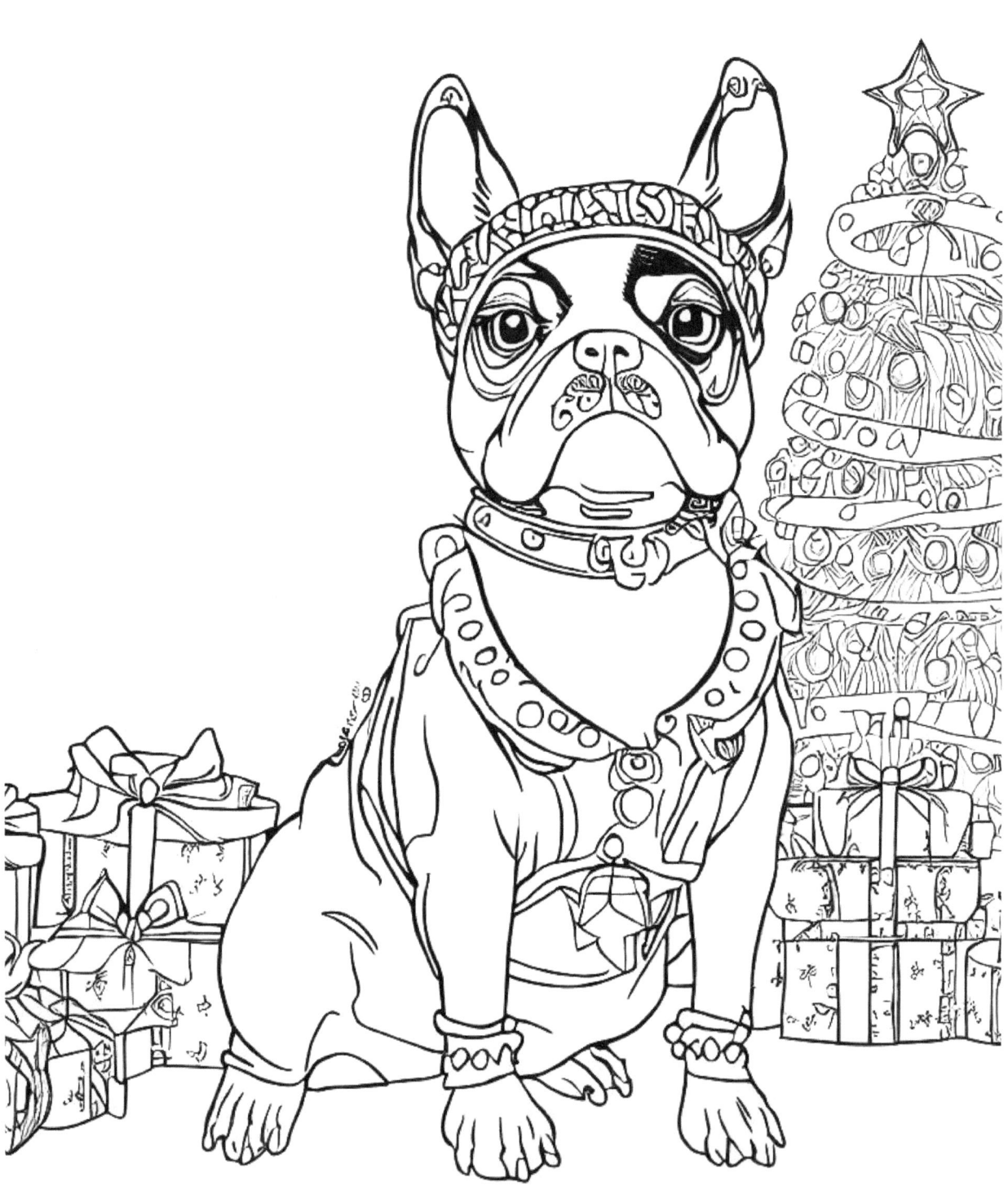

✤ Bulldog

Bulldogs are furry, with wrinkled face so sweet,
Their wagging tails bring joy, their love is hard to beat.
They're cuddly pals for kids, a playful bundle of fun,
With every wag and snuggle, a friendship has begun.

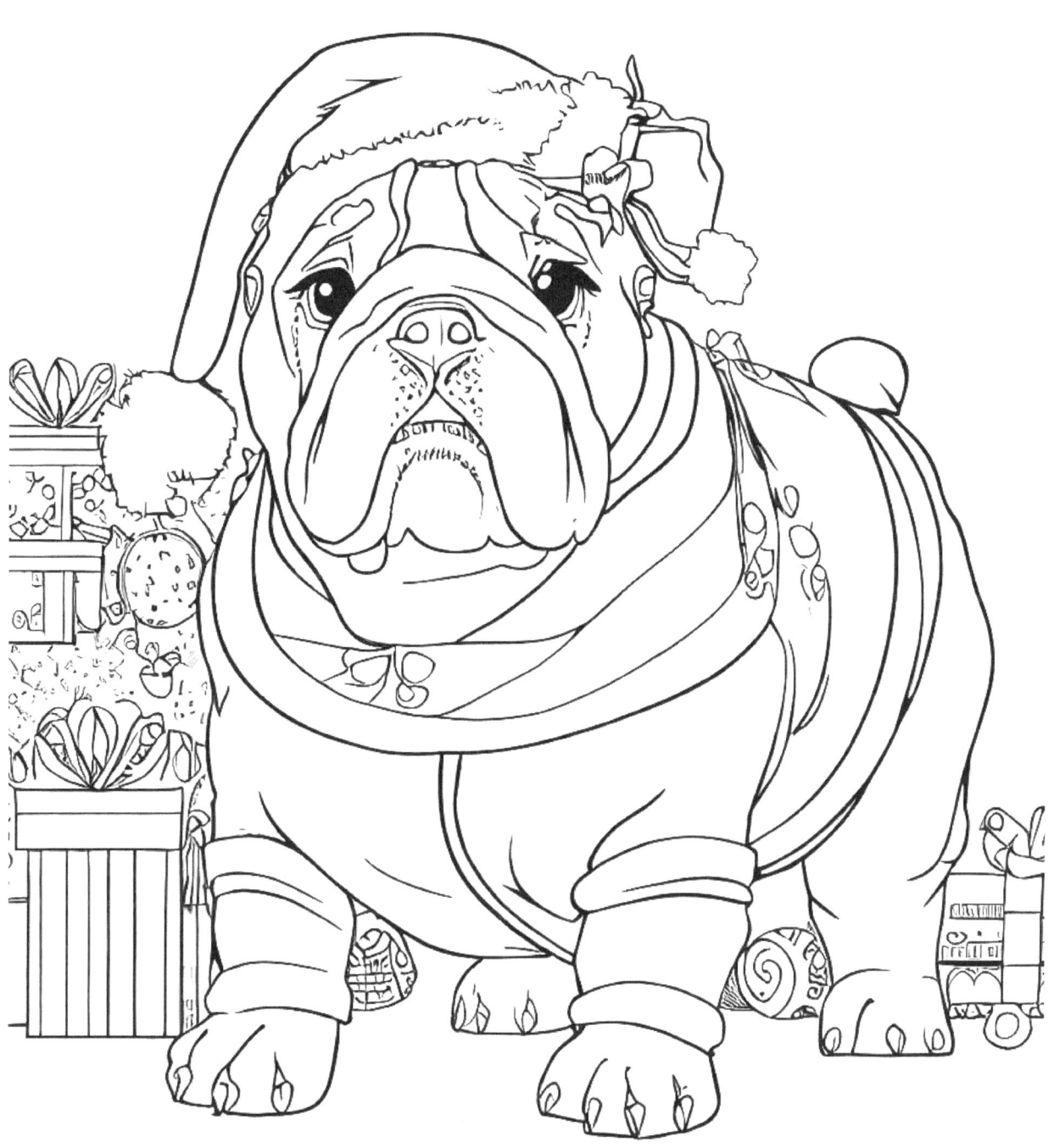

❀ Bull Terrier

With a muscular stance and a spirit so bright,
The Bull Terrier plays with all its might.
Egg-shaped head and eyes full of fire,
A loyal companion that never tires.

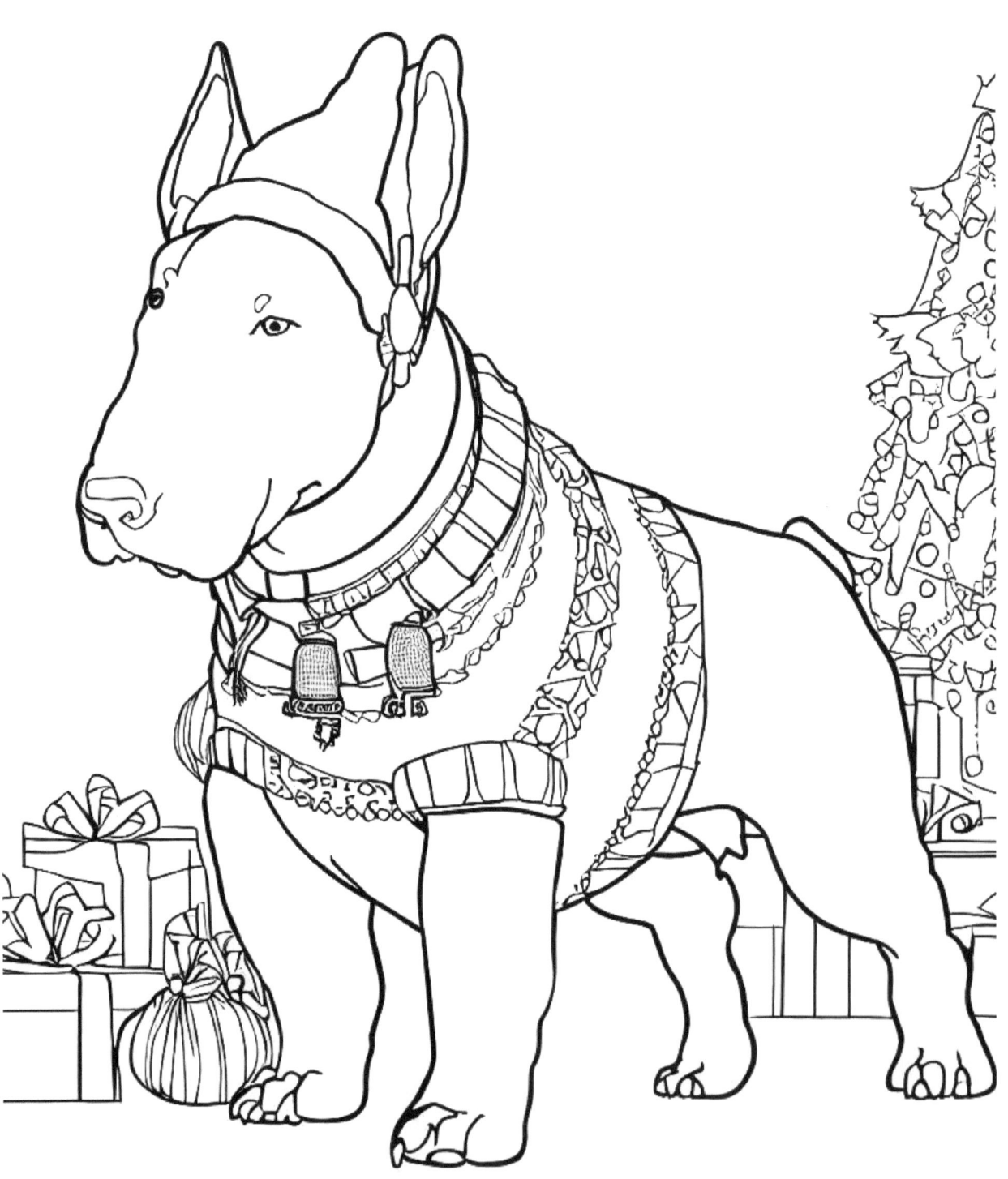

❋ Cavalier King Charles Spaniel

With elegant ears and a gentle gaze,
Cavaliers steal your heart in a daze.
Their royal name suits them well,
In their company, happiness will swell.

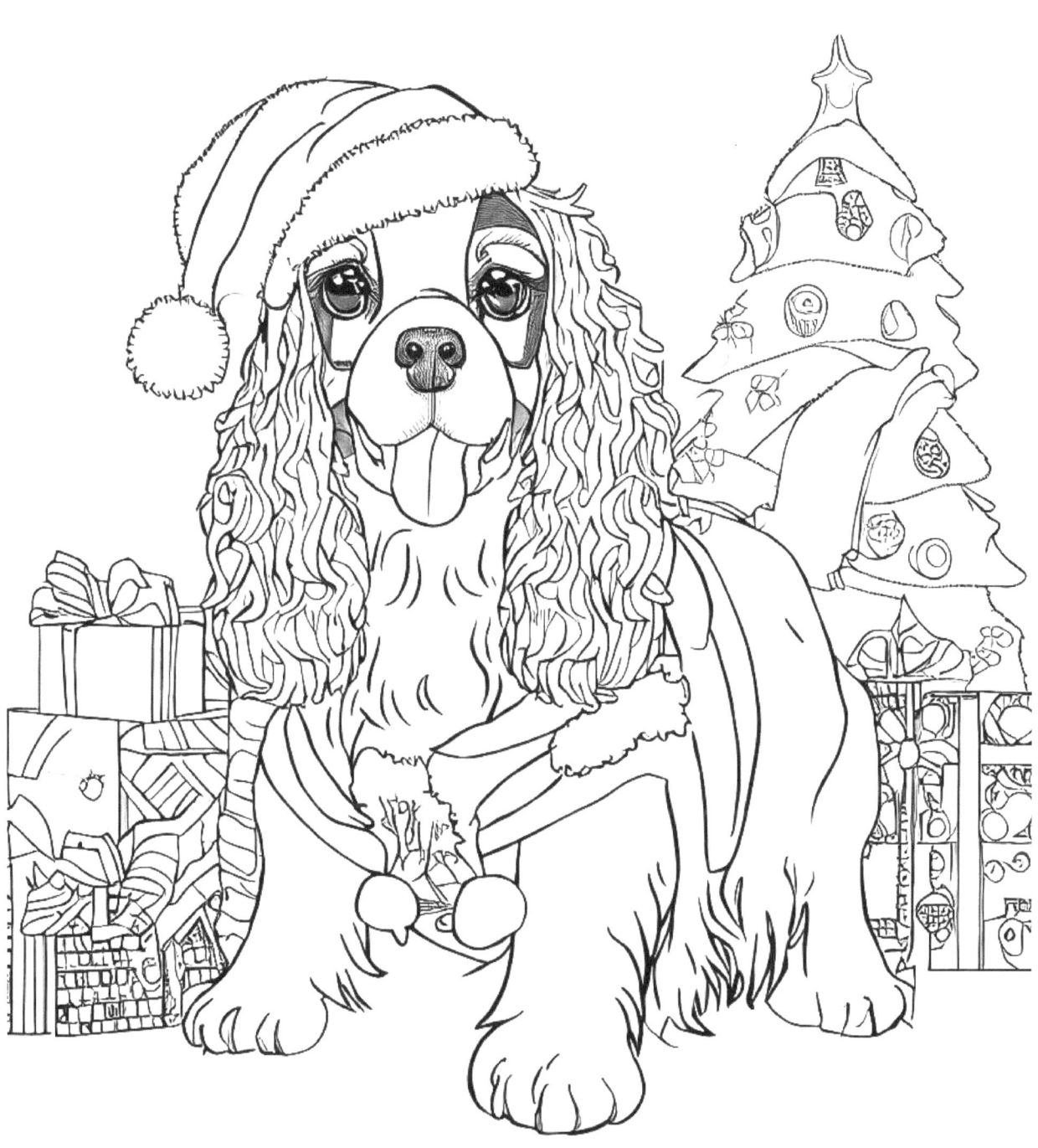

❁ Chihuahua

Tiny and *fierce*, a pocket-sized star,
Chihuahua's spirit shines near and far.
Bold in attitude, with a heart so true,
A pint-sized friend who's always there for you.

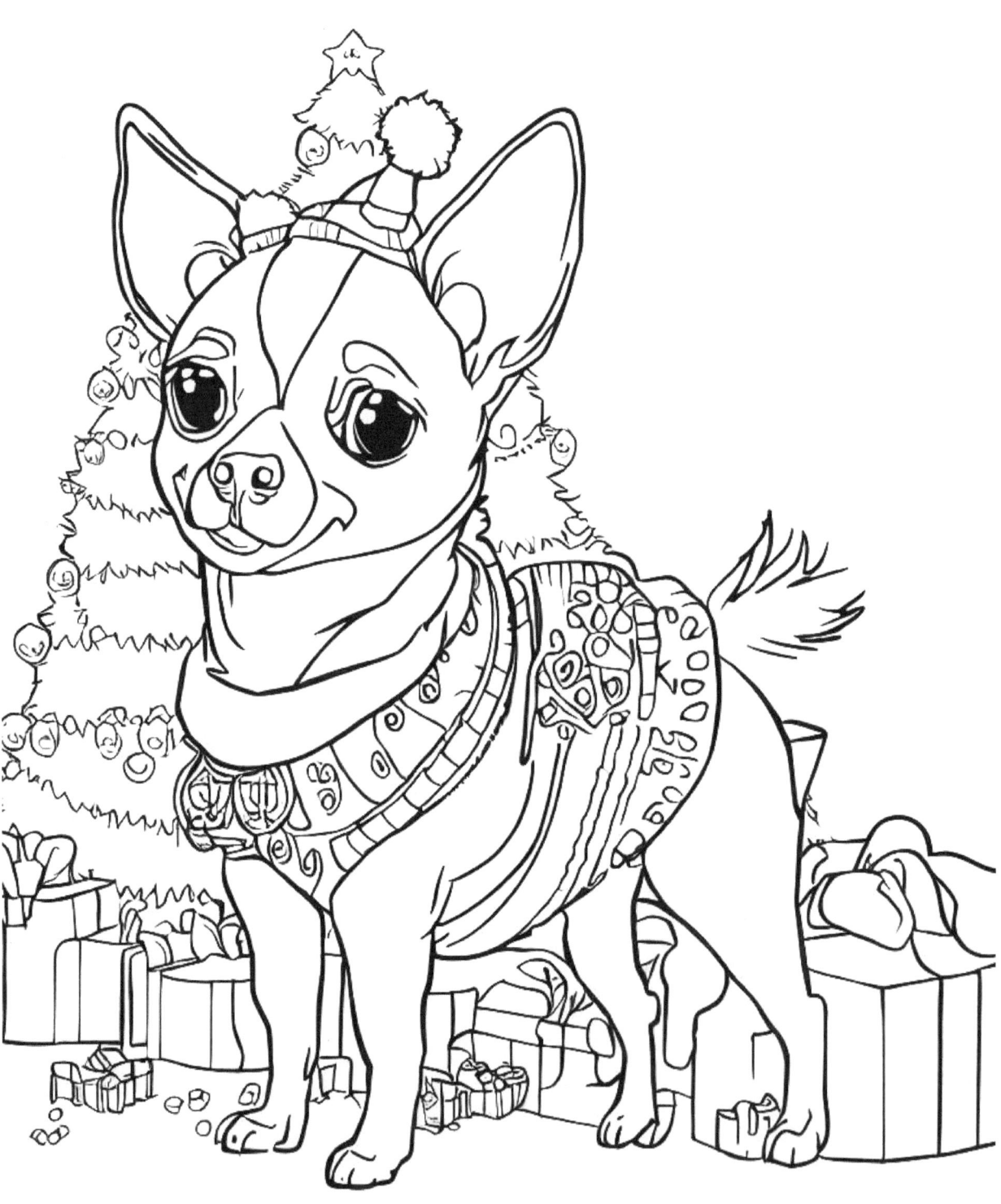

Cocker Spaniel

Eyes like gems that sparkle and gleam,
Cocker Spaniel's charm is quite the dream.
With flowing ears and a wagging tail,
A joyful companion on every trail.

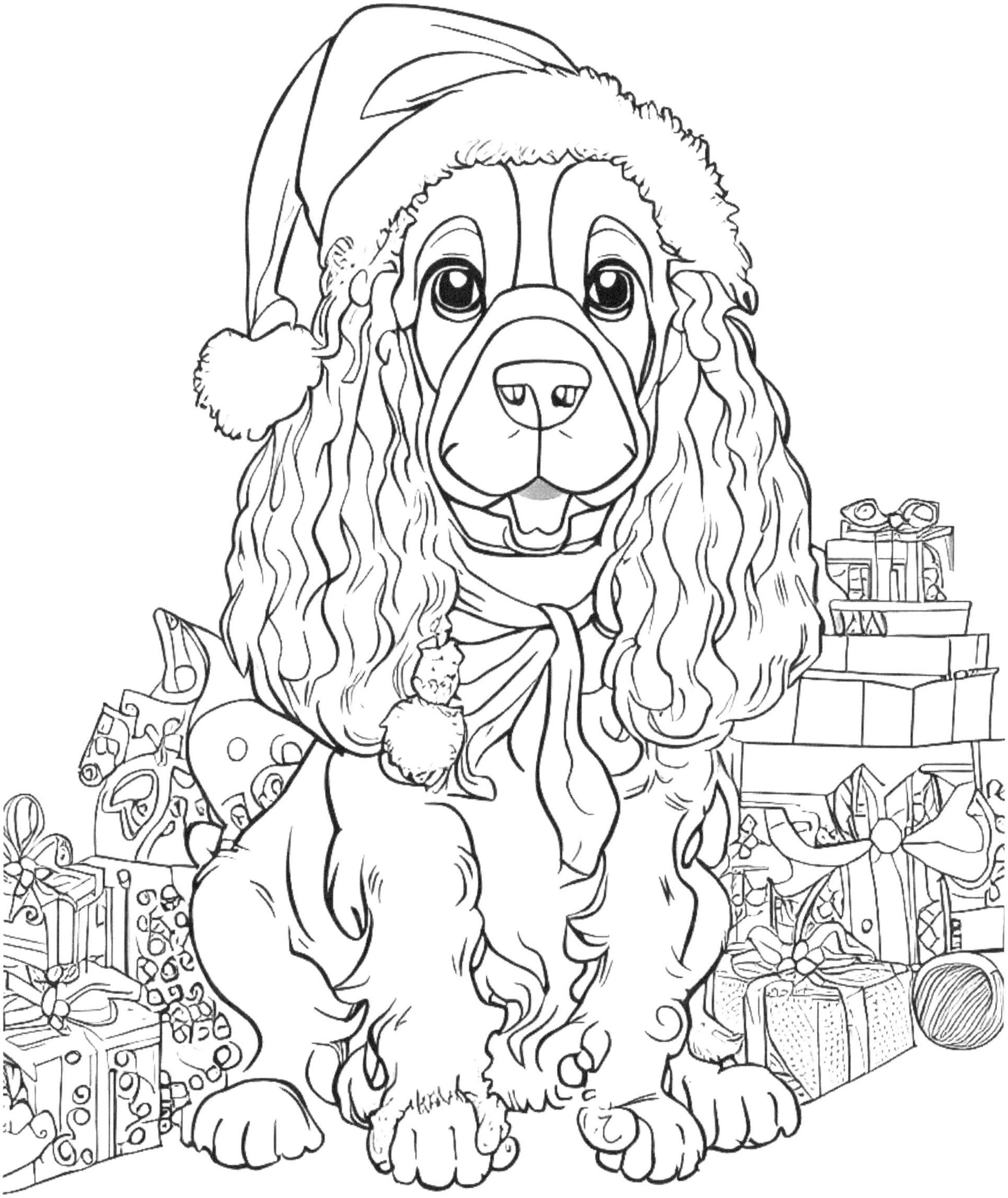

🐾 Corgi

Short legs and a heart so big,
Corgi's energy is like a lively jig.
Bounding with joy, a royal delight,
A loyal friend from morning to night.

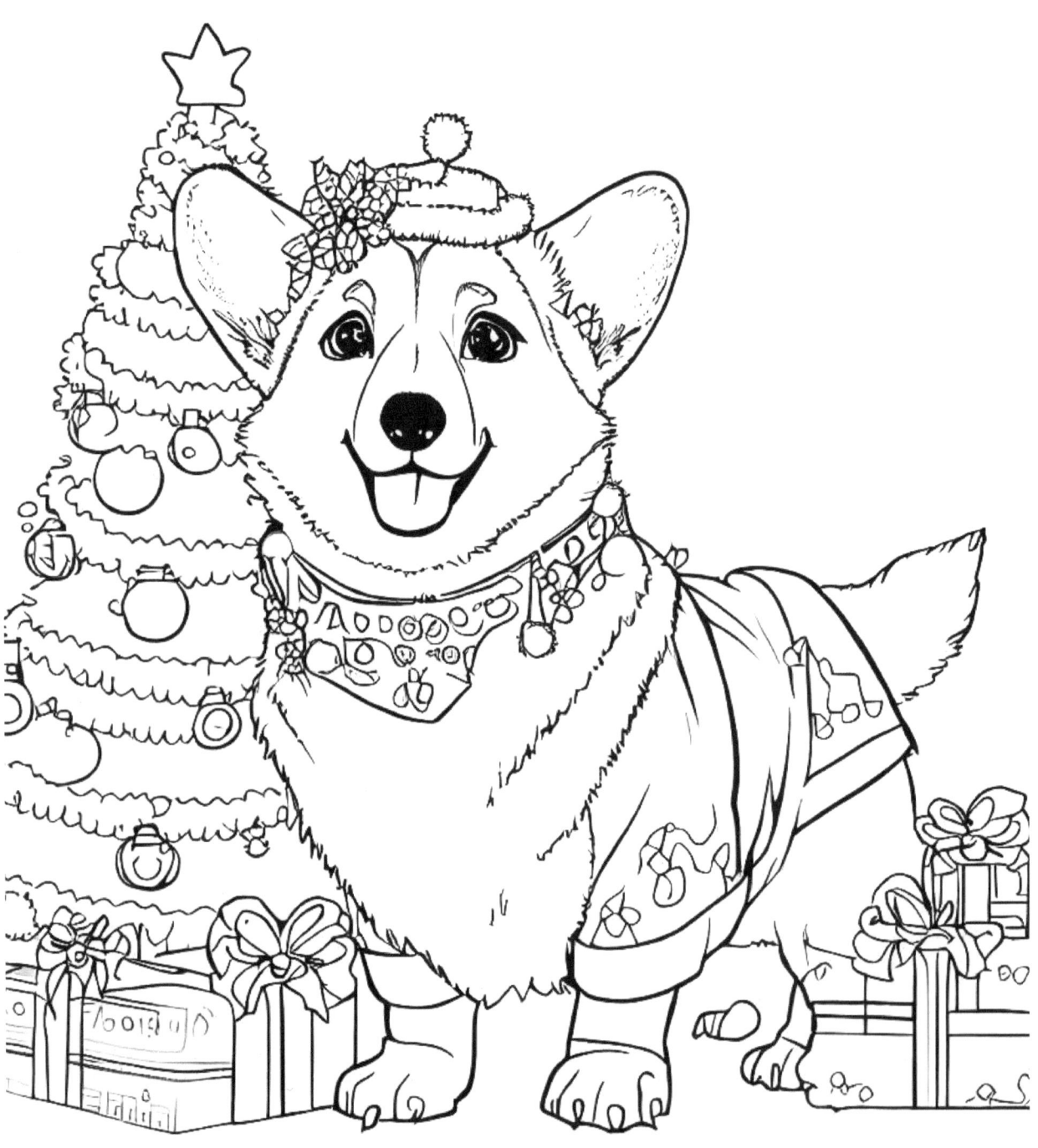

✤ Dachshund

Long and low, with a spunky stride,
Dachshund's loyalty cannot hide.
They'll dig into your heart so deep,
In their love, you'll take a leap.

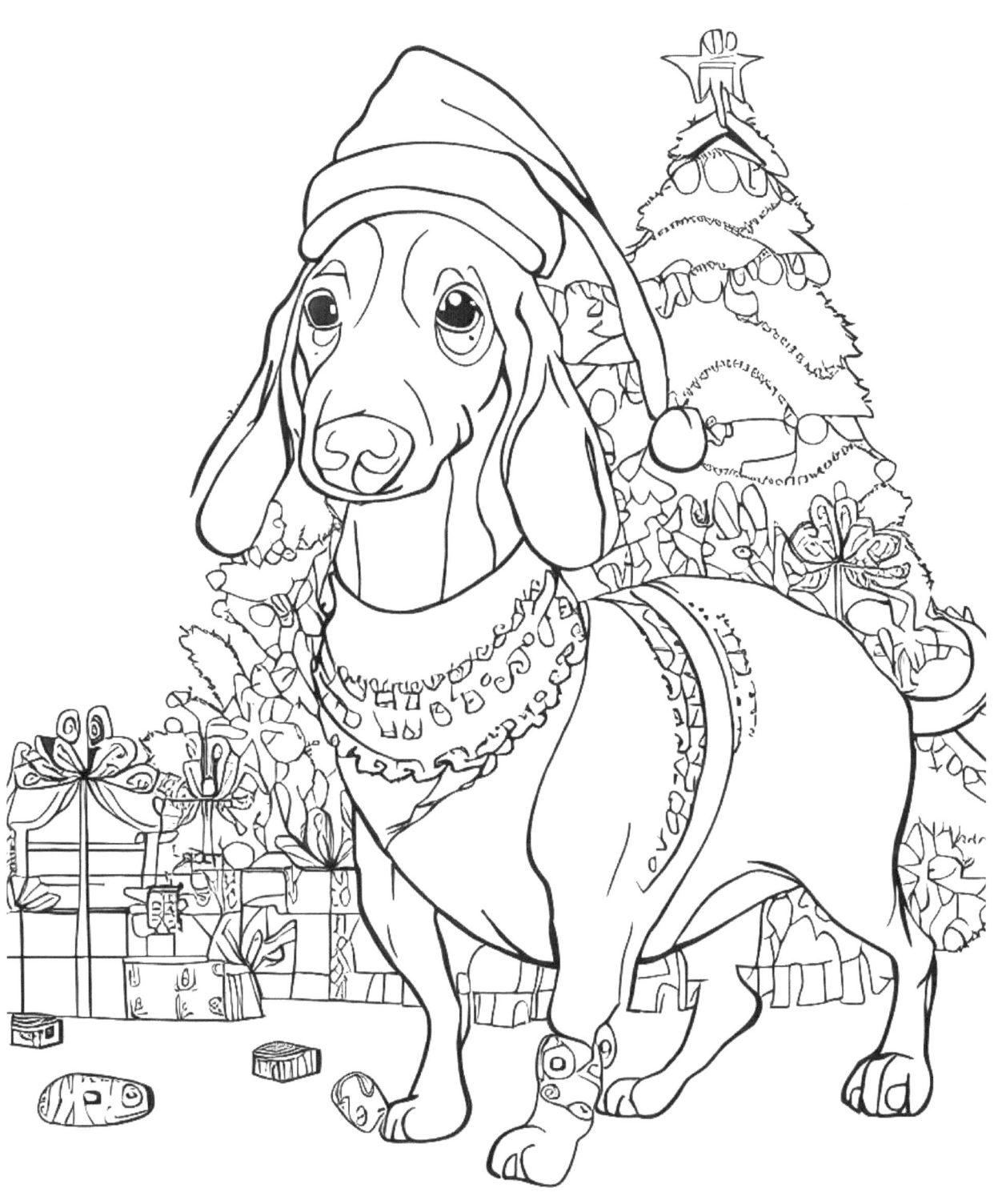

❧ Dalmatian

Spots of black on coats so white,
Dalmatian's energy is pure delight.
With every bound, they'll make you smile,
A companion who goes the extra mile.

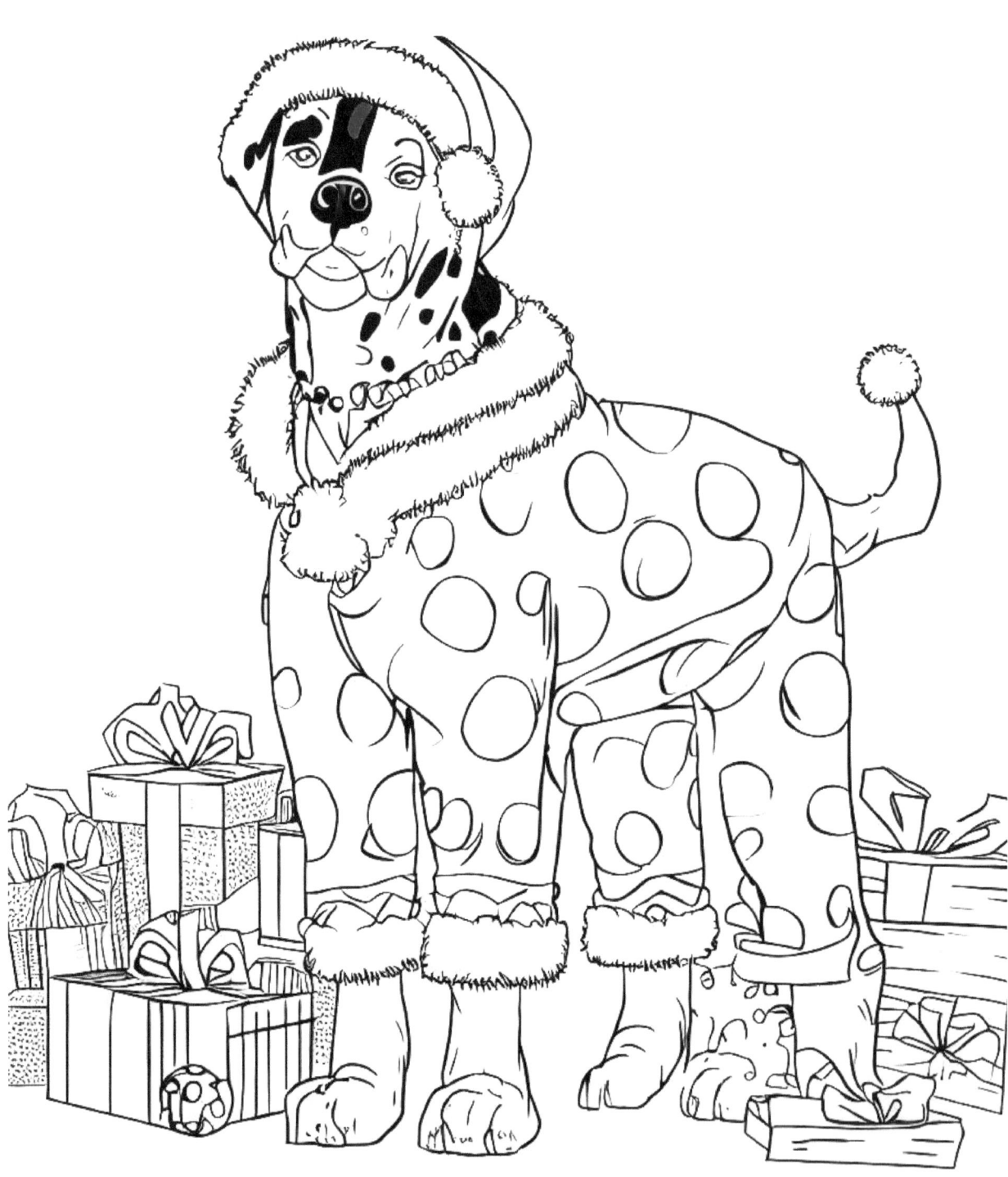

❀Doberman Pinscher

Elegance meets strength, sleek and bold,
Doberman's heart is made of gold.
A guardian, loyal and true,
They'll protect and cherish you.

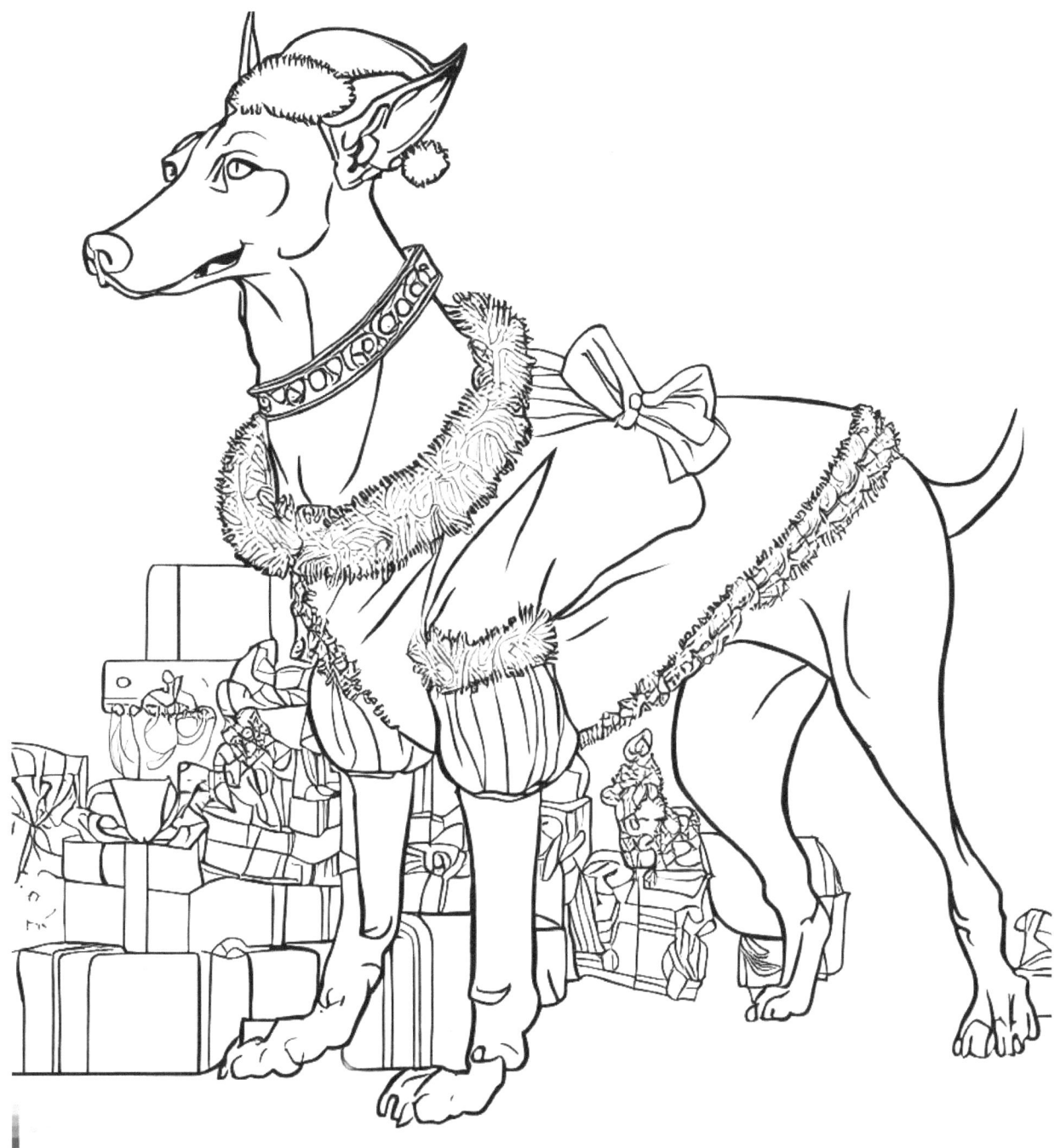

🐾 French Bulldog

In Parisian cafes, the Frenchie is cool,
With ears like batwings, never acting dull.
Small but so spunky, with a joyful cheer,
A playful best friend bringing smiles near.

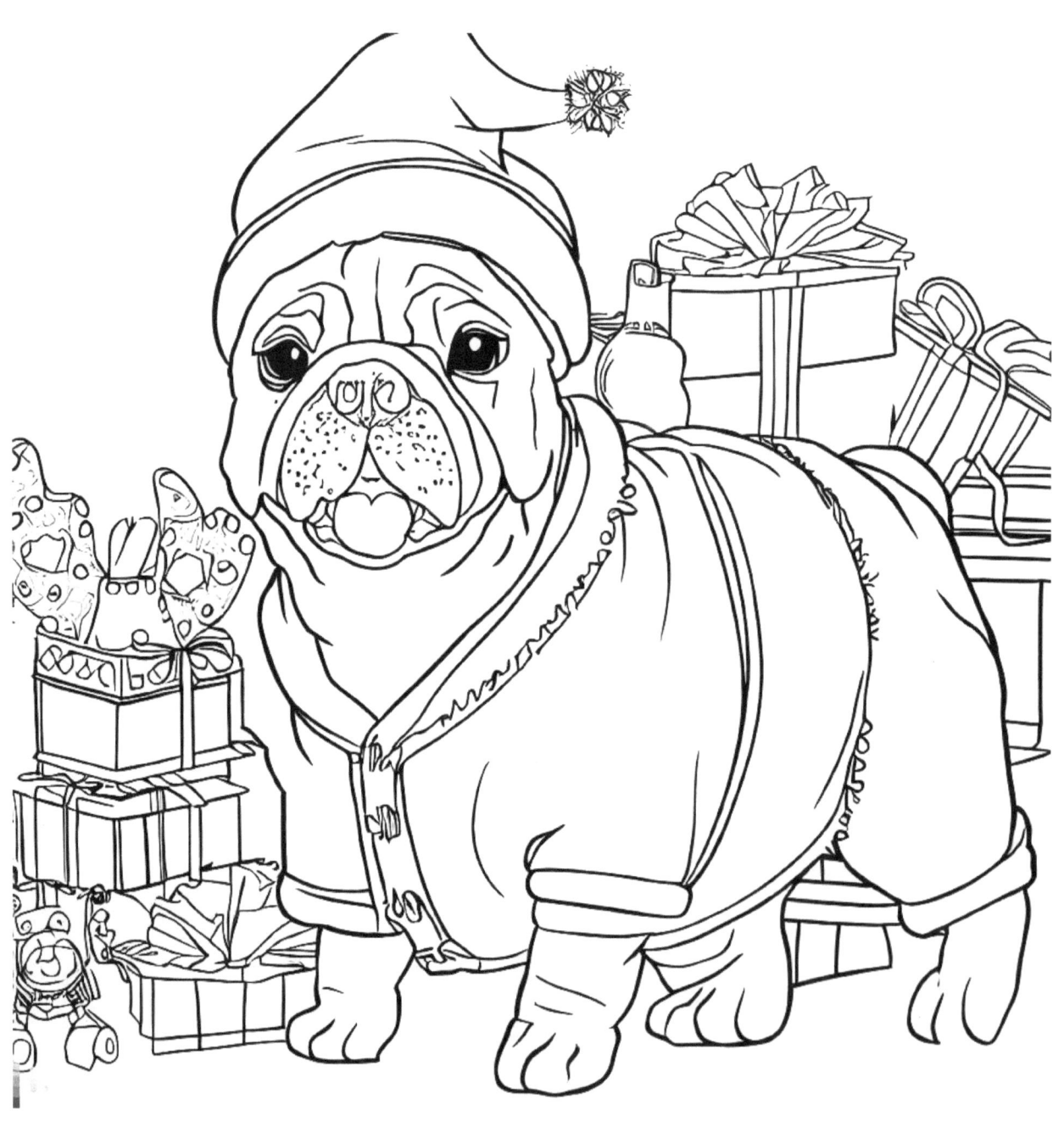

✿ German Shepherd

Intelligence and loyalty unite,
German Shepherd, a guardian's light.
They'll stand by your side, brave and strong,
A friend who'll never steer you wrong.

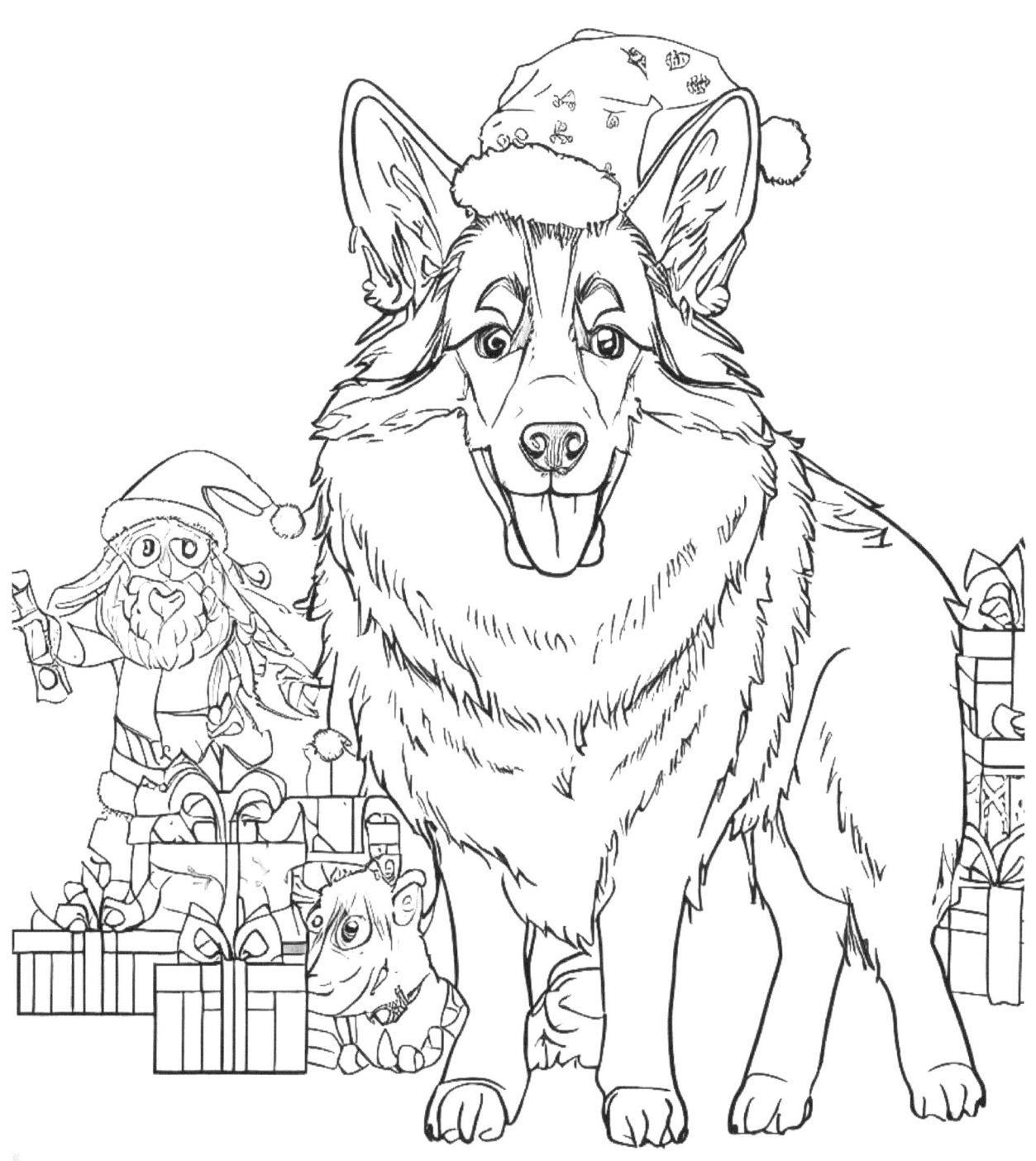

❀ Golden Retriever

Golden fur and eyes so warm,
Golden Retriever, a soothing charm.
Their hearts are filled with love untold,
In their presence, you'll never feel old.

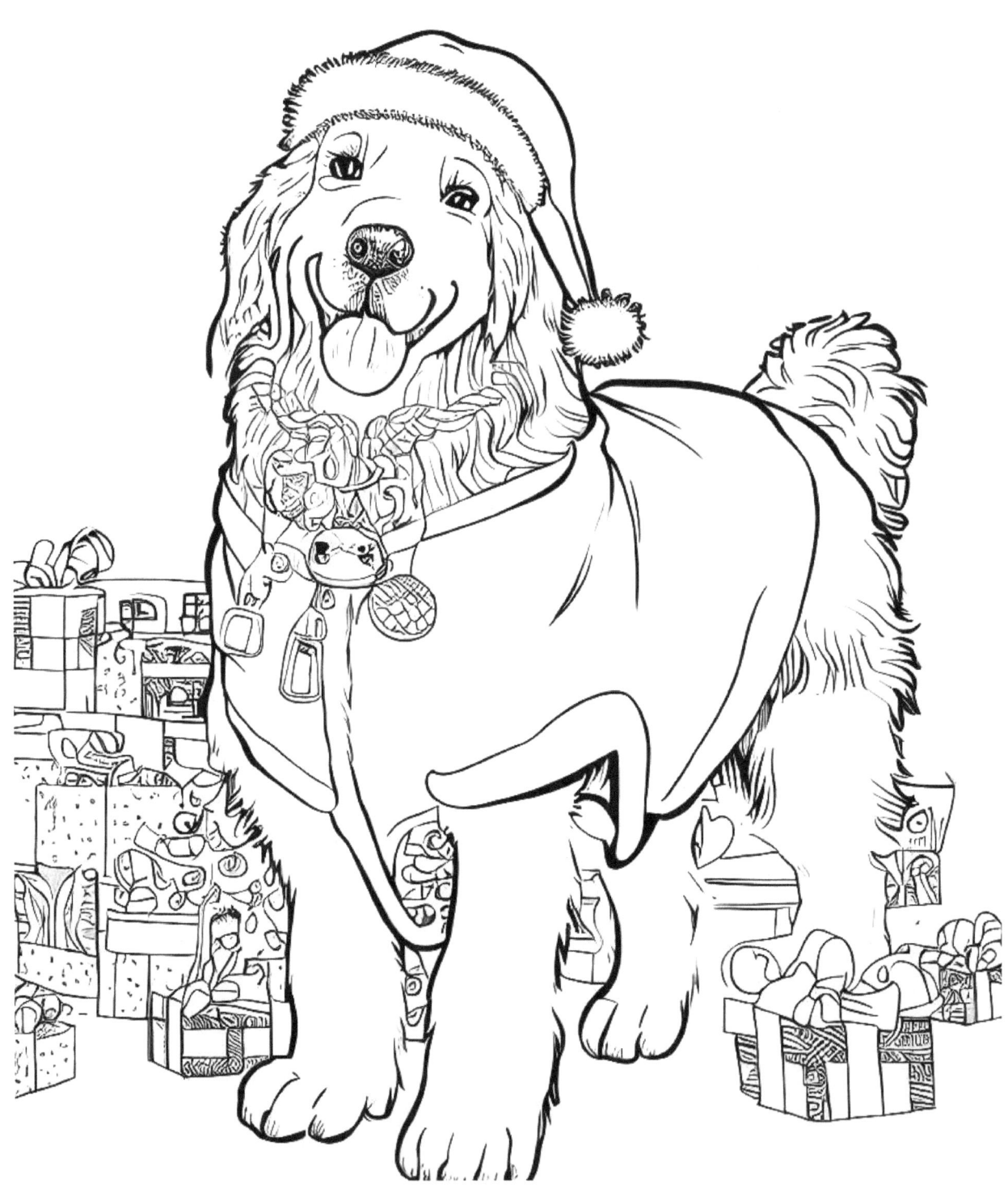

❀ Great Dane

Towering and gentle, giants they are,
Great Dane's love will take you far.
With a heart as large as their towering stance,
They'll bring joy and love in abundance.

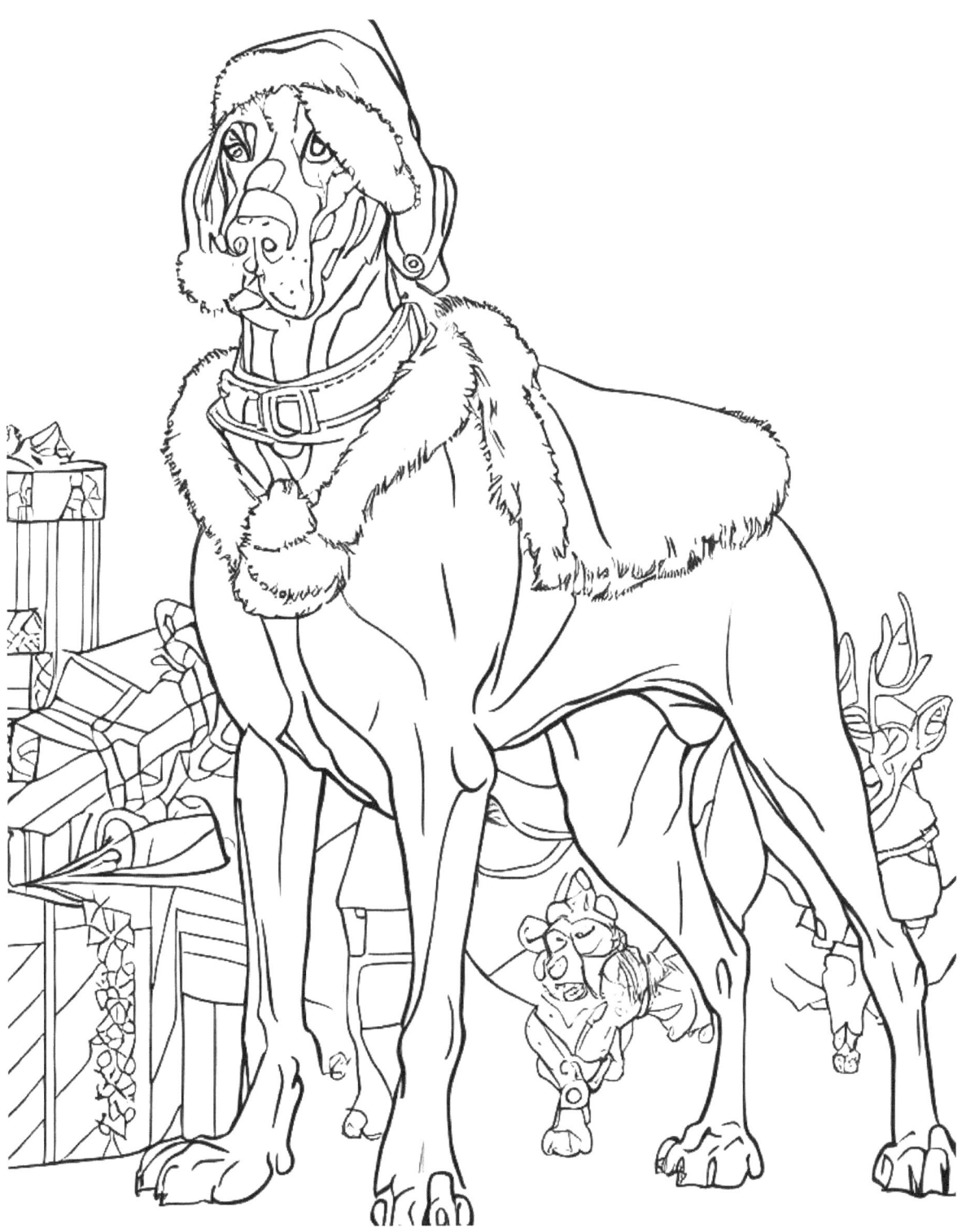

🐾 Havanese

Silky coat and joyful cheer,
Havanese will bring you near.
With a bounce and a wagging tail,
In their love, you'll set sail.

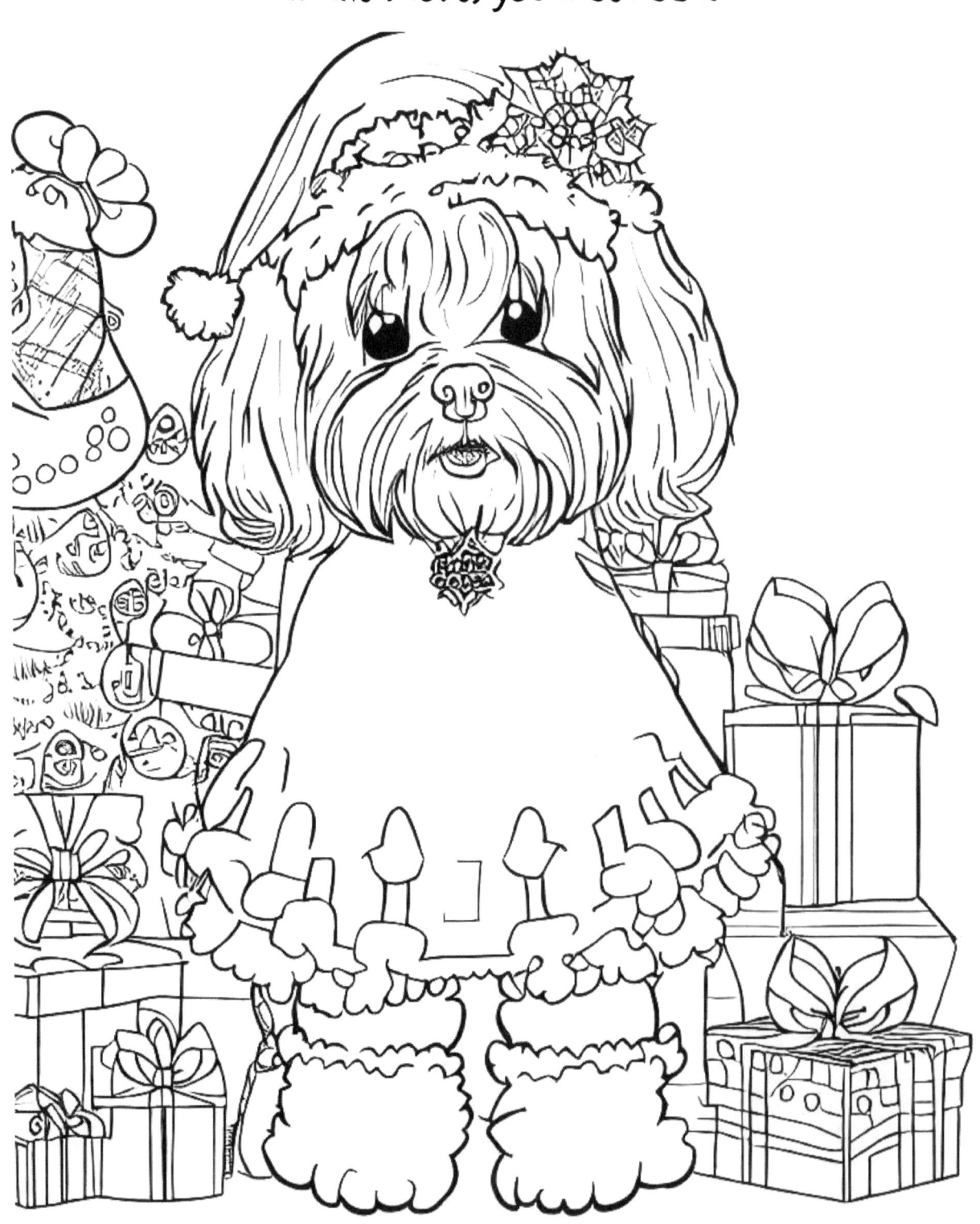

❀ Maltese

Fluffy and white, like a cloud so light,
Maltese's love is pure and bright.
With every skip and loving gaze,
They'll brighten up your days.

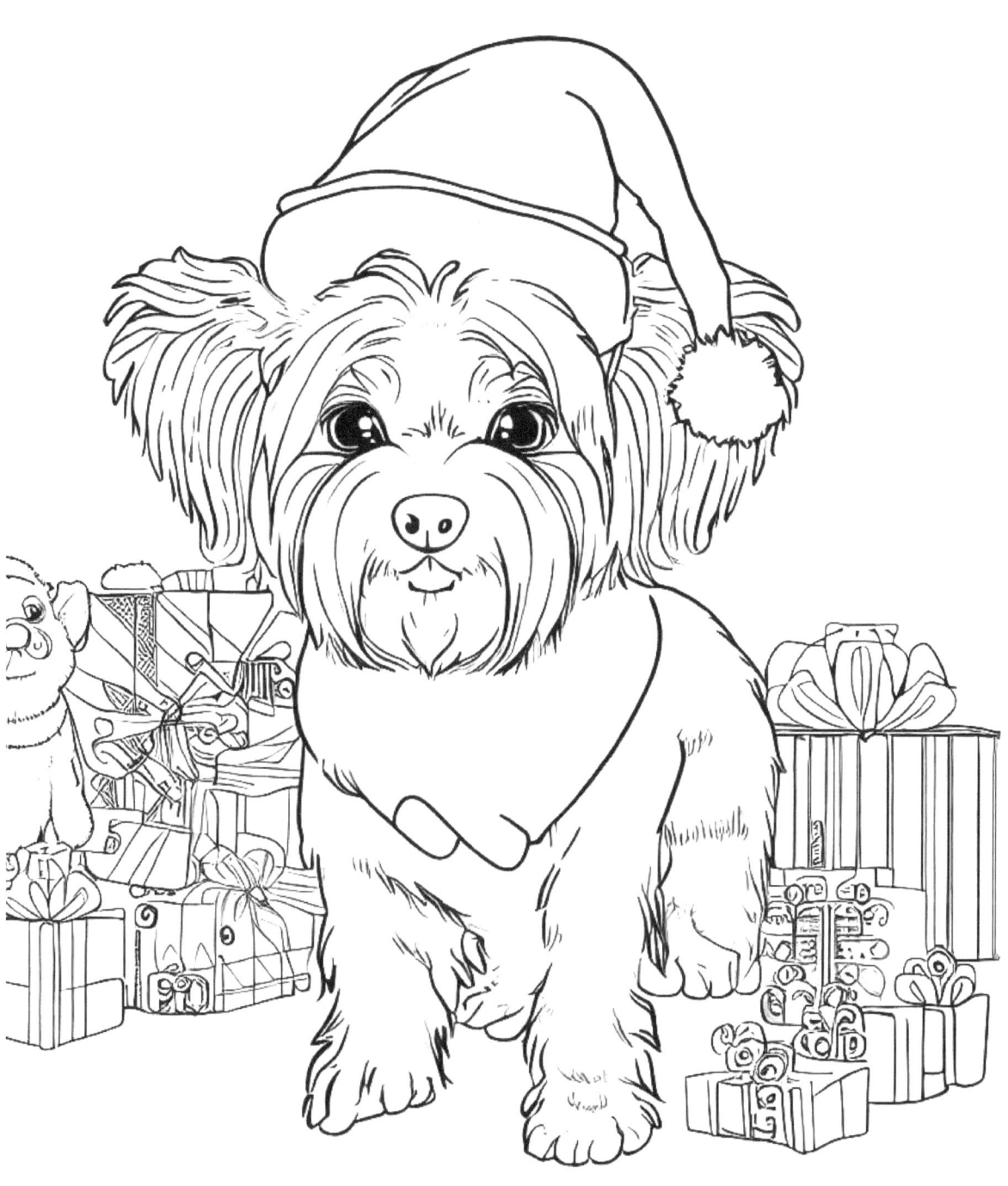

❀ Newfoundland

Gentle giant, kind and sweet,
Newfoundland's love is a soothing beat.
They'll rescue your heart from any storm,
A loyal companion in any form.

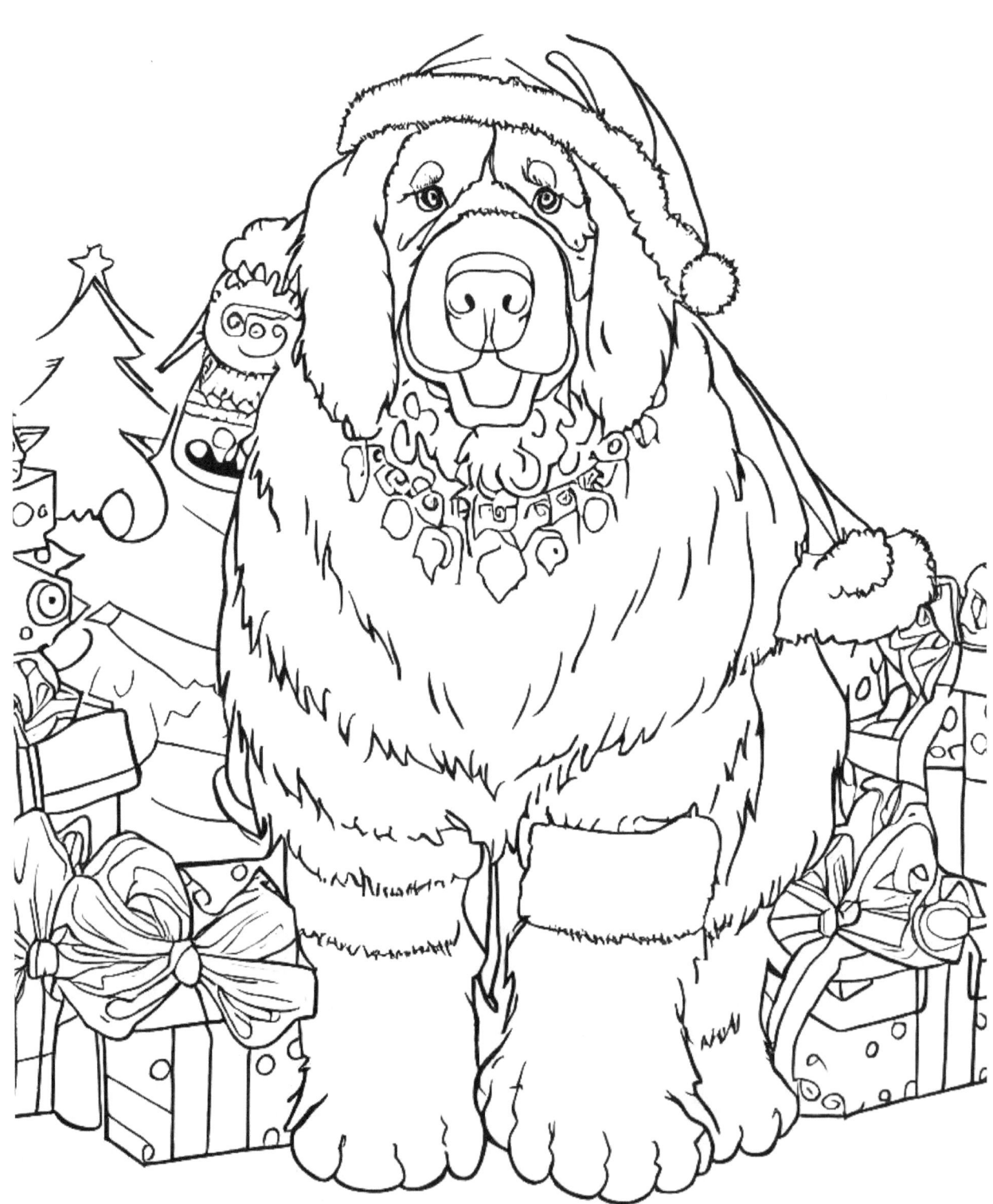

🐾 Papillon

Ears like butterfly wings, they soar,
Papillon's love is worth much more.
With a prance and a joyful flip,
They'll bring delight with every trip.

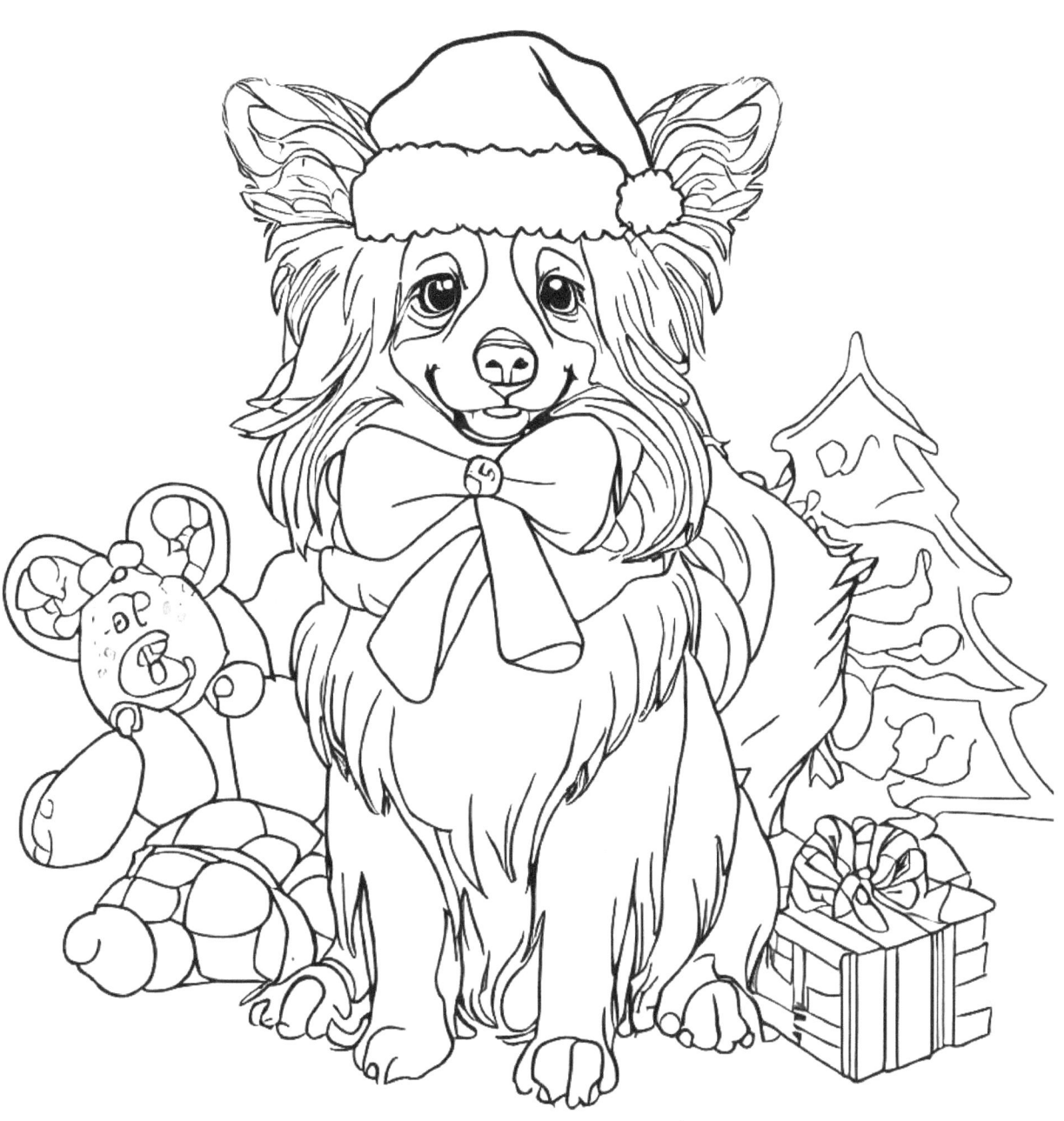

🐾 Pekingese

Regal in stance and a lion's mane,
Pekingese's love will never wane.
With a dignified and tender grace,
They'll hold a special, cherished place.

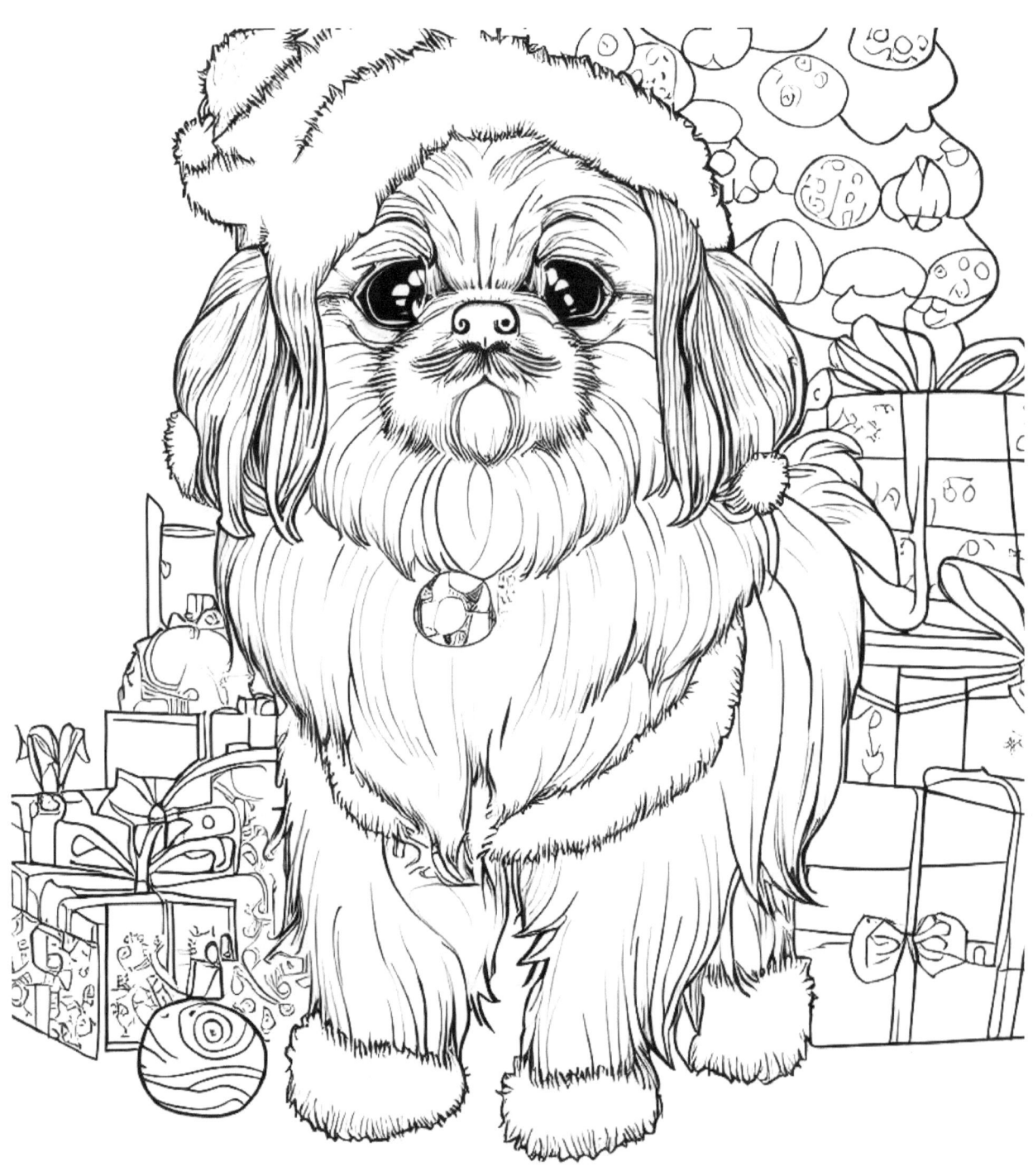

❀ Pomeranian

Fluffy and bright, like a burst of sun,
Pomeranian's love is always fun.
With a yip and a playful spin,
They'll wrap your heart from deep within.

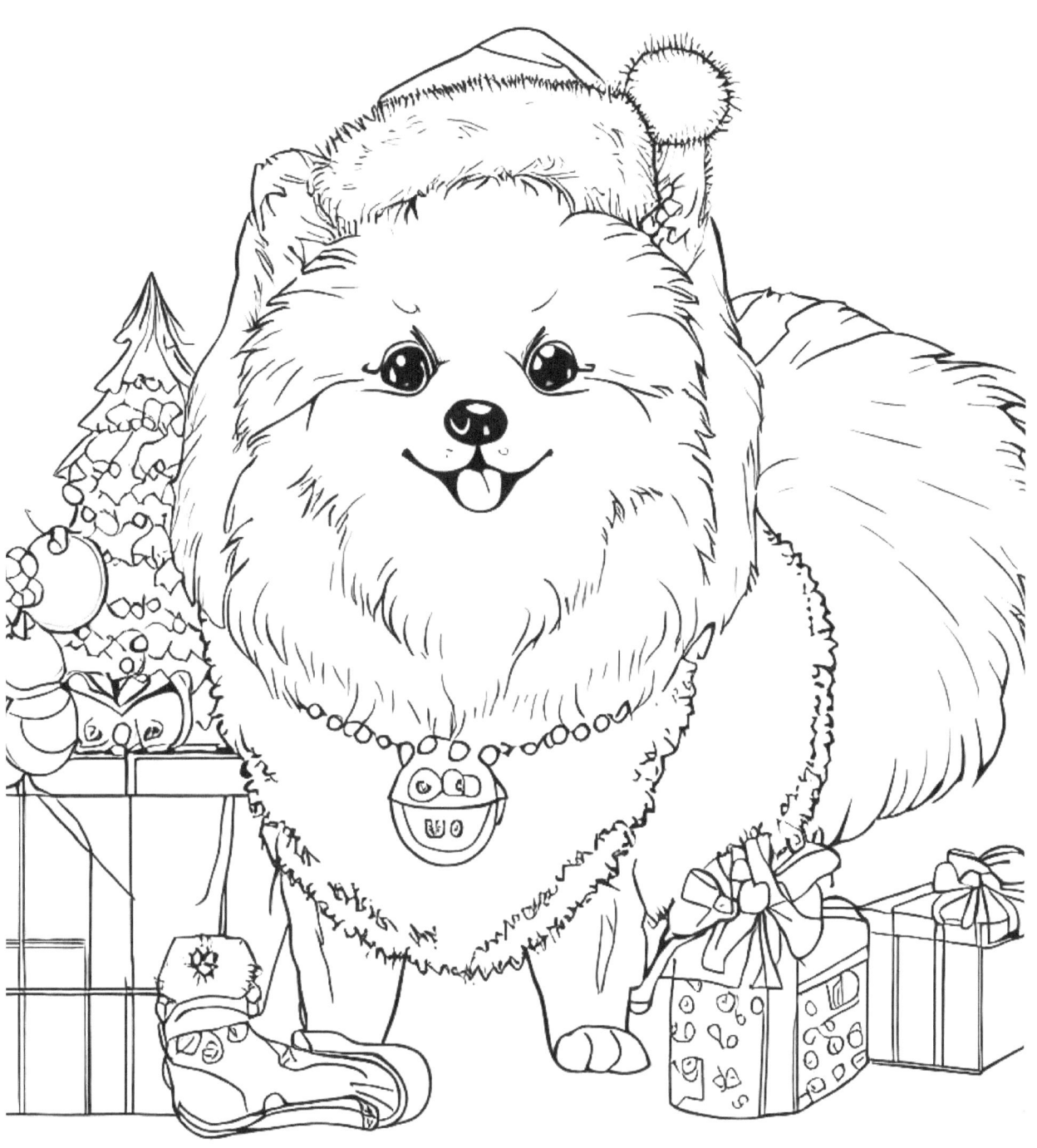

🐾 Poodle

Fluffy or sleek, they come in style,
Poodle's love makes you smile.
With intelligence and a joyful heart,
They'll be your friend from the start.

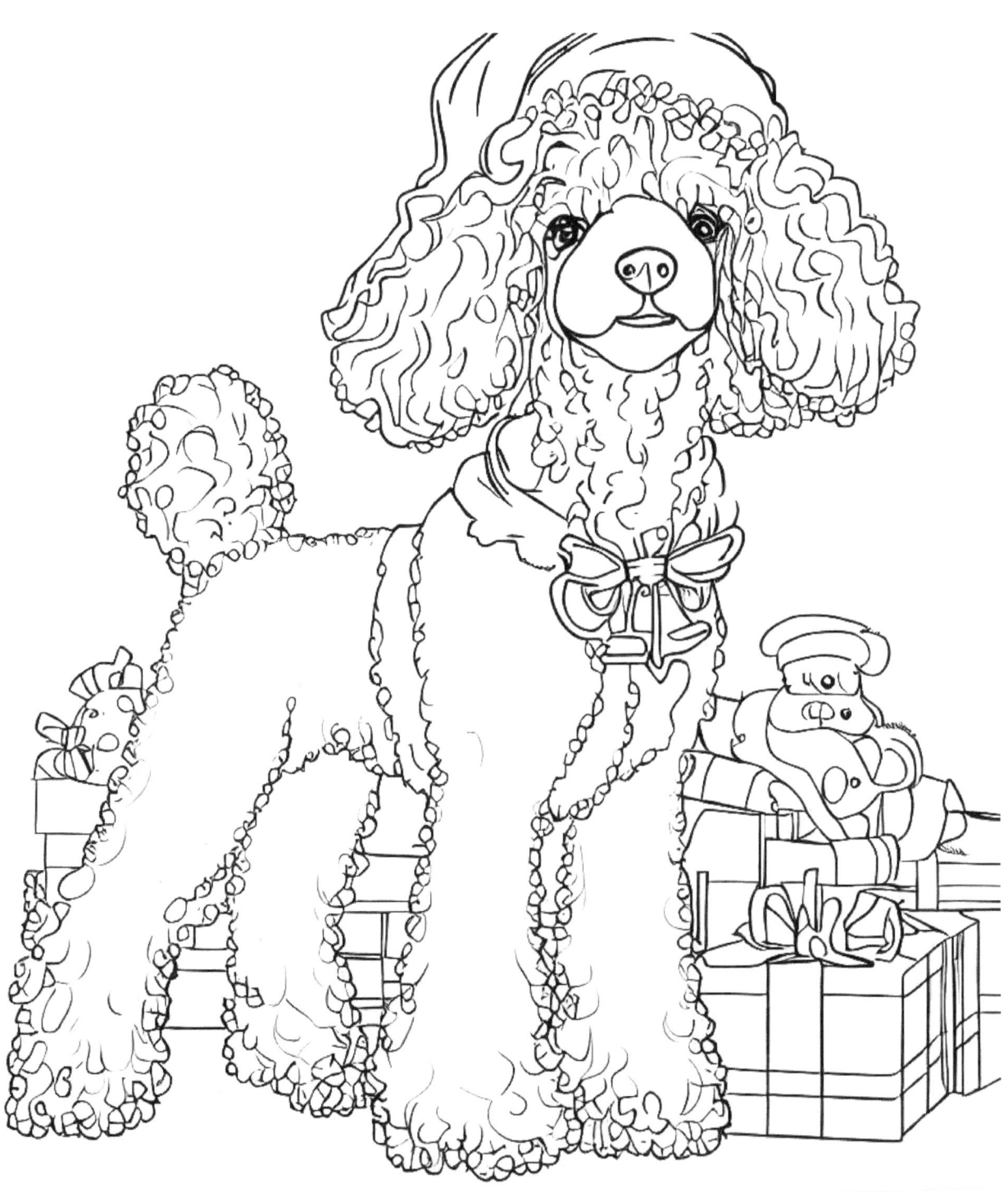

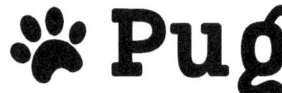 Pug

wrinkled face and eyes so wide,
Pug's love is a constant tide.
with every snort and playful nudge,
They'll be your friend, never a grudge.

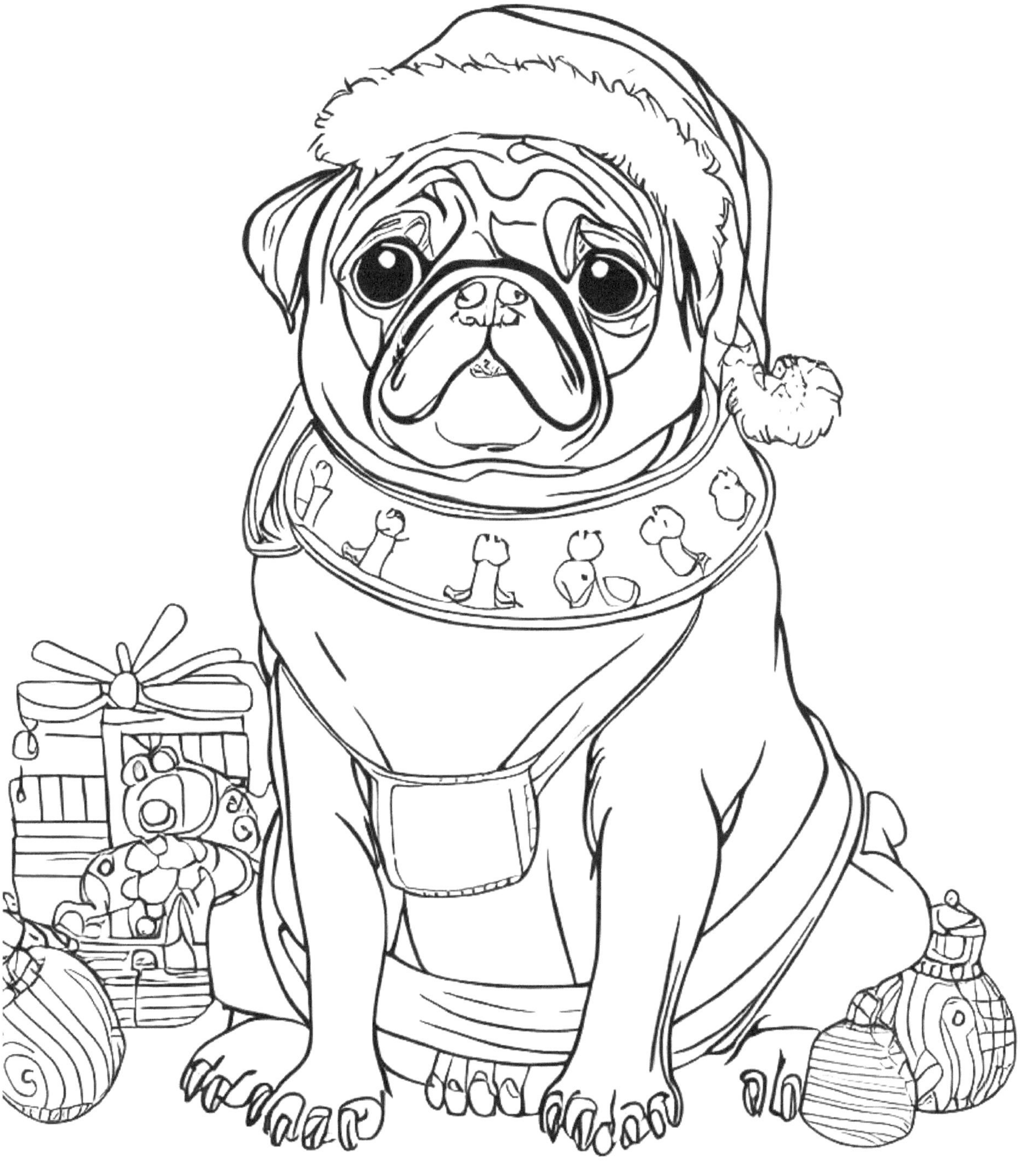

🐾 Samoyed

Fluffy as snow and a smile so bright,
Samoyed's love is pure delight.
With every bounce and a joyful bark,
They'll light up your life, even in the dark.

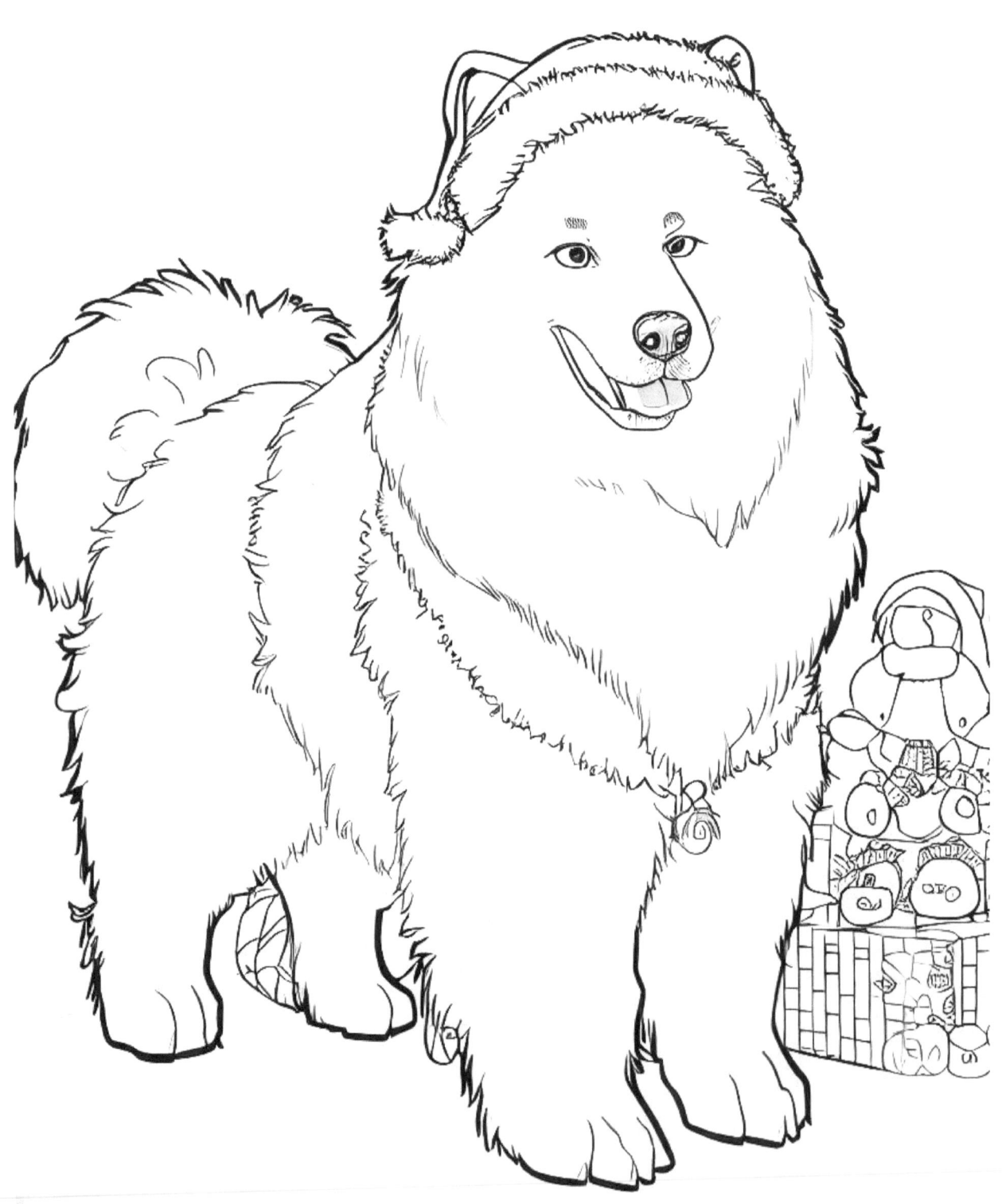

✿Schnauzer

Whiskered face and eyes so wise,
Schnauzer's love is a sweet surprise.
With a regal stance and loyalty so deep,
They'll be your friend, your secrets to keep.

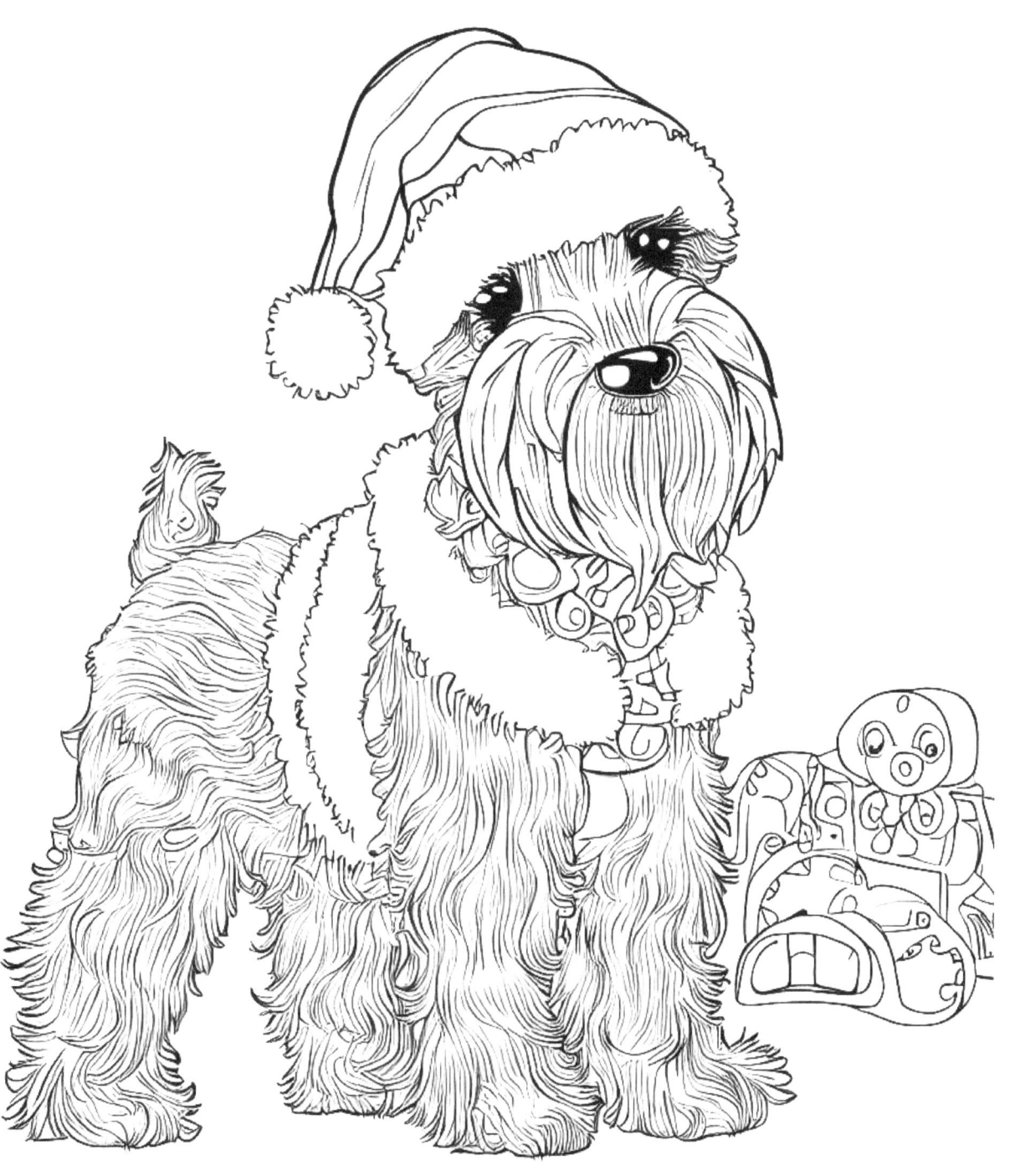

❀ St. Bernard

A gentle giant with a heart so grand,
St. Bernard lends a helping hand.
In snowy landscapes, they proudly roam,
Rescue heroes leading lost souls home.

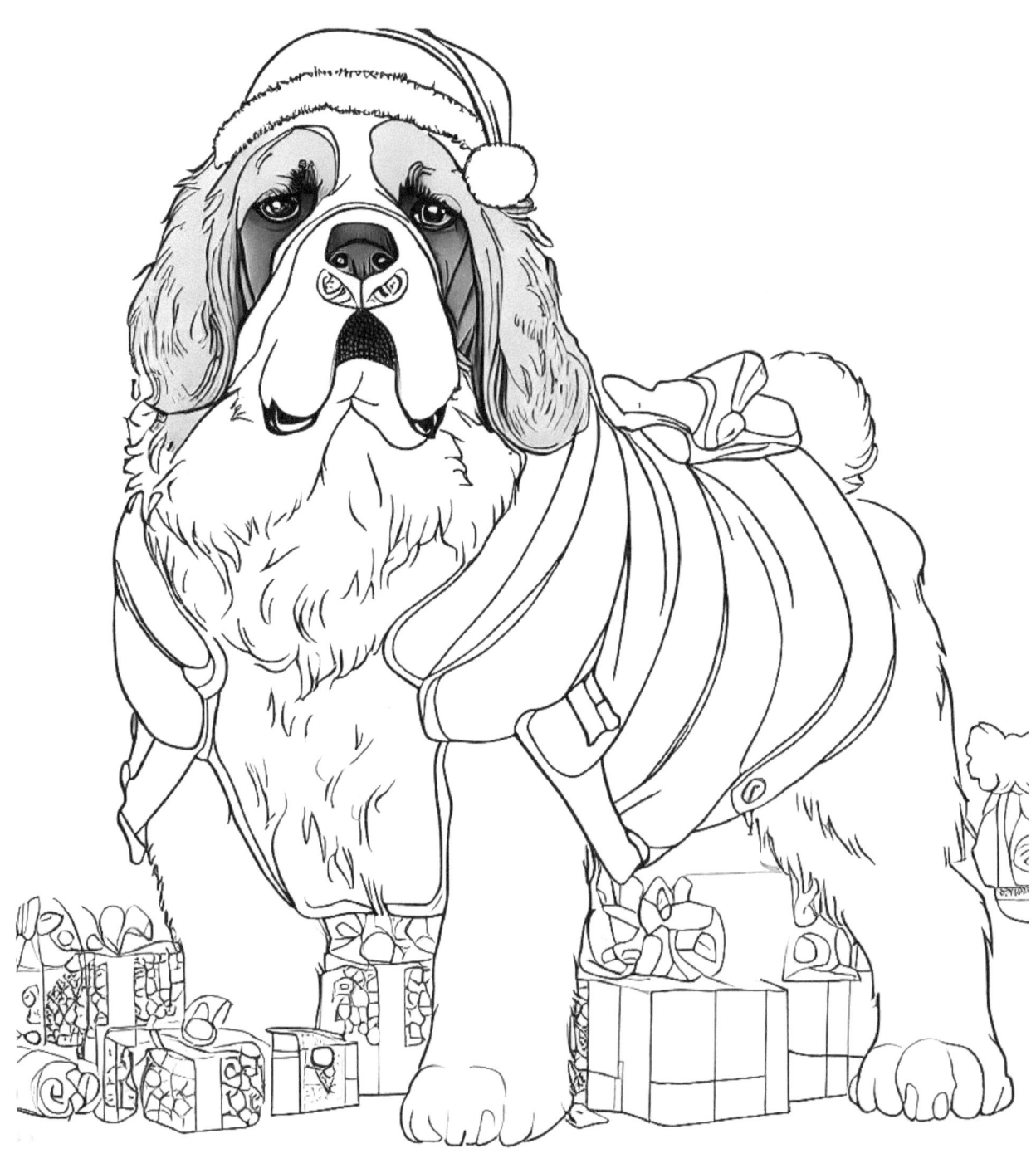

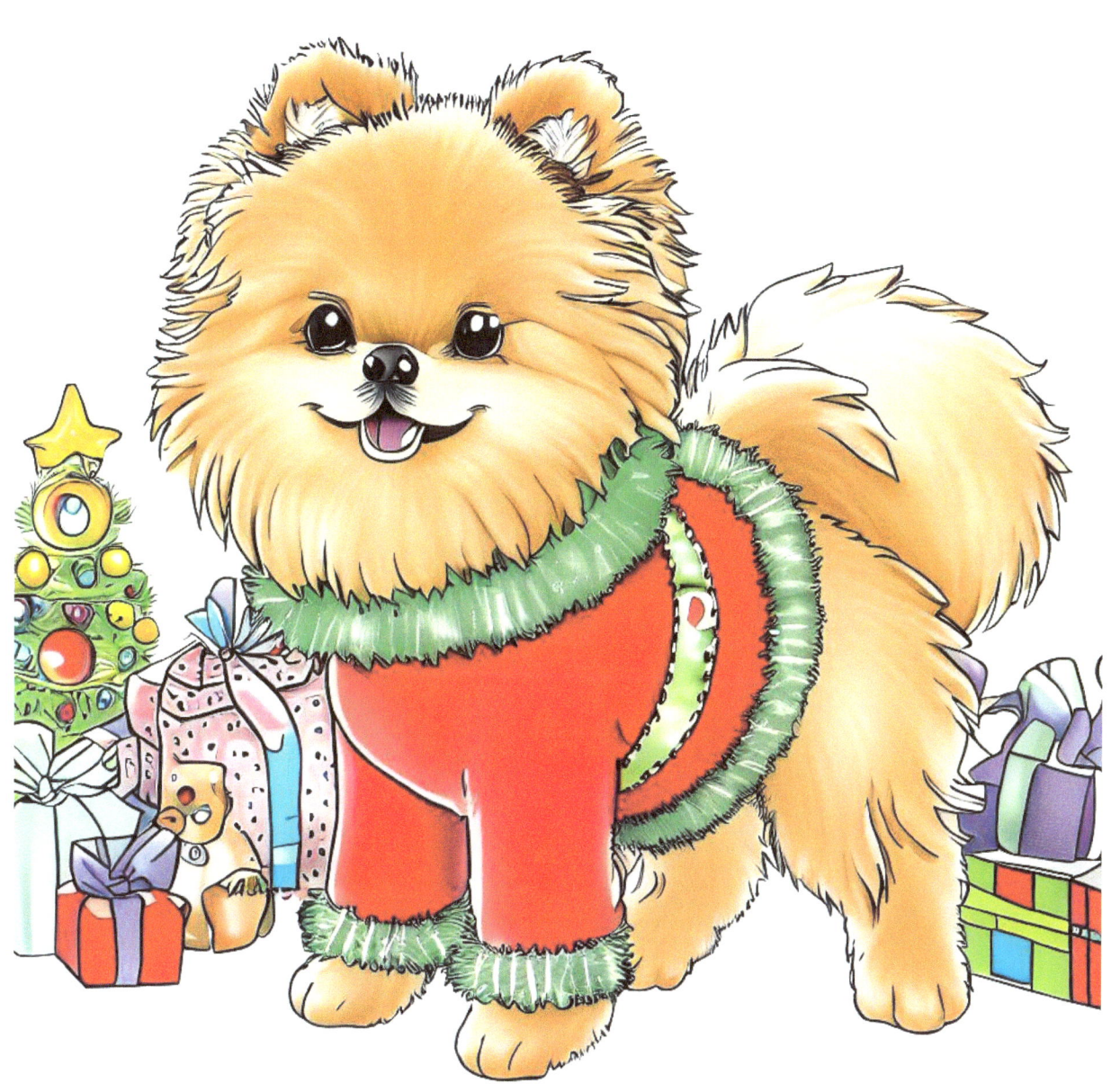

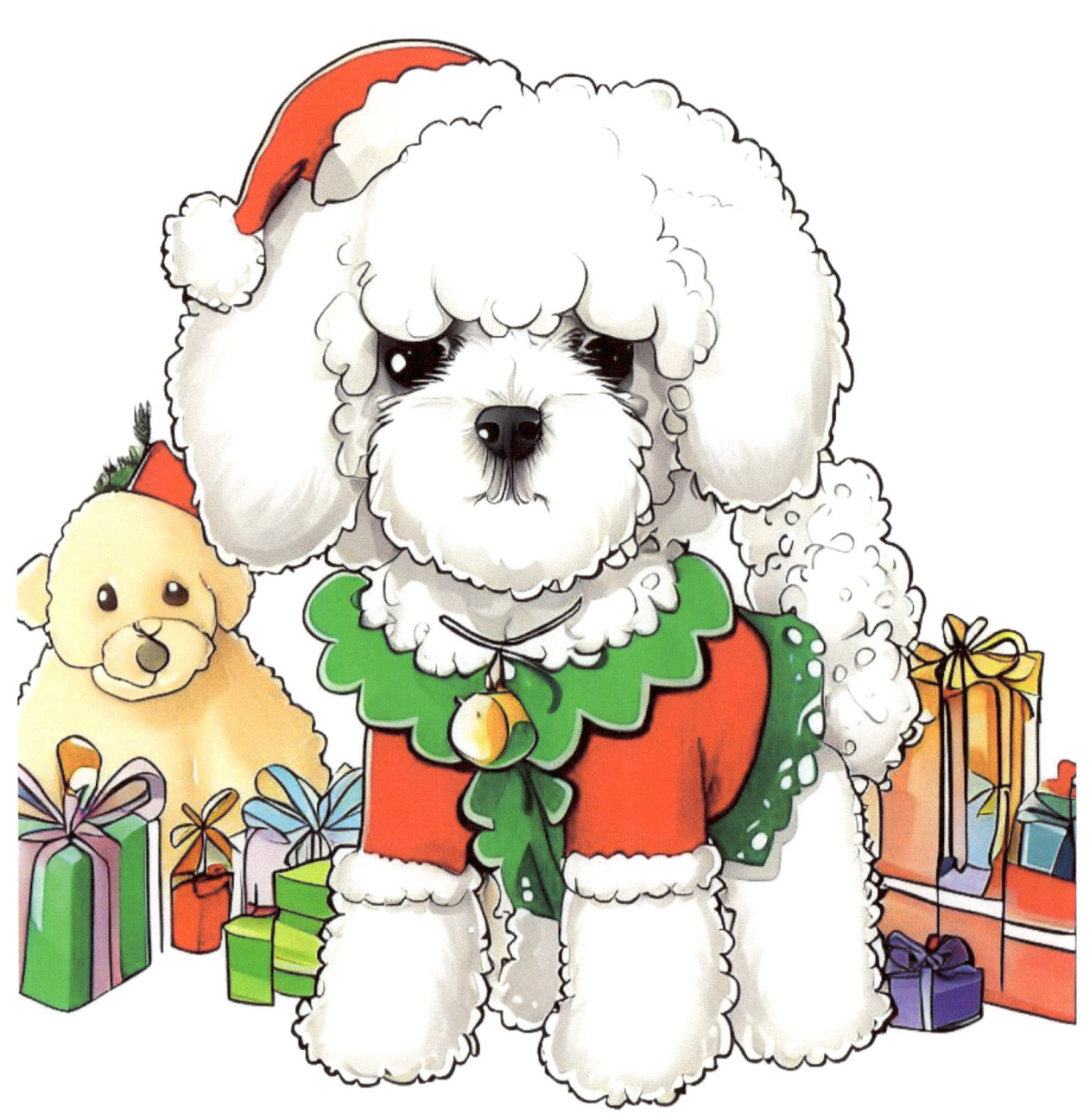